COMMUNITIES
■ NEAR <u>AND</u> FAR ■

There are many different kinds of communities. Some are large and some are small. They have different kinds of houses. What is your community like?

BARRY K. BEYER

JEAN CRAVEN

MARY A. McFARLAND

WALTER C. PARKER

MACMILLAN/McGRAW-HILL SCHOOL PUBLISHING COMPANY

NEW YORK CHICAGO COLUMBUS

PROGRAM AUTHORS

Dr. Barry K. Beyer
Professor of Education and American Studies
George Mason University
Fairfax, Virginia

Jean Craven
Social Studies Coordinator
Albuquerque Public Schools
Albuquerque, New Mexico

Dr. Mary A. McFarland
Instructional Coordinator of Social Studies,
 K-12 and Director of Staff Development
Parkway School District
Chesterfield, Missouri

Dr. Walter C. Parker
Associate Professor, College of Education
University of Washington
Seattle, Washington

CONTENT CONSULTANTS

Reading
Dr. Virginia Arnold
Senior Author, *Connections* Reading Program
Richmond, Virginia

Economics
Dr. George Dawson
Professor of Economics
Empire State University
Bellmore, New York

Special Populations
Dr. Jeannette Fleischner
Professor of Education
Teachers College
Columbia University
New York, New York

Curriculum
John Sanford
Director of Curriculum
Acalanes Union High School District
Lafayette, California

Multicultural
Dr. Joe Trotter
Professor of History
Carnegie Mellon University
Pittsburgh, Pennsylvania

History
Dr. David Van Tassel
Founder of United States History Week
Professor of History
Case Western Reserve University
Cleveland, Ohio

Geography
Nancy Winter
Member of the Executive Board of the
 National Council for Geographic Education
Social Studies Teacher
Bedford, Massachusetts

International Education
Gary Yee
Principal
Hillcrest School
Oakland, California

GRADE-LEVEL CONSULTANTS

Lynette Arnold
Elementary Teacher
Westwood Primary School
Phoenix, Arizona

Pamela Crowell
Elementary Teacher
Badin Elementary School
Badin, North Carolina

Louise Dunn
Elementary Teacher
Baileyton Elementary School
Greenville, Tennessee

Angelina Gonzalez
Elementary Teacher
Fremont Elementary School
Alhambra, California

Jo-Ann Potter
Elementary Teacher
North Hero Elementary School
North Hero, Vermont

Jonathan Powell
Elementary Teacher
Emerson Open Magnet School
Wichita, Kansas

CONTRIBUTING WRITER

Linda Scher
Raleigh, North Carolina

ACKNOWLEDGMENTS

The publisher gratefully acknowledges permission to reprint the following copyrighted material:
"Revolutionary Tea" words by Seba Smith and music by H. D. Munson appears in SPECTRUM OF MUSIC,
Grade 3—Mary Val Marsh, Carroll Rinehart and Edith Savage, Senior Authors (New York: Macmillan, 1983).
Excerpt from "Little Blue Top" by Tony Hughes from POLLUTION OR ECOLOGY. Copyright © 1970 Lutheran
Church Press. Reprinted by permission of Augsburg Fortress. Excerpt from OF PLYMOUTH PLANTATION by
William Bradford edited by Samuel Eliot Morison. Copyright 1952 by Alfred A. Knopf, Inc. Used by permission
of the publisher.

Macmillan/McGraw-Hill School Division
866 Third Avenue
New York, New York 10022

Printed in the United States of America
ISBN 0-02-145903-7
9 8 7 6 5 4 3

CONTENTS

SPECIAL SECTION 278

REFERENCE SECTION 297

Building Citizenship

Building Skills

Charts, Graphs, Diagrams, and Time Lines

Maps

USING YOUR TEXTBOOK

TABLE OF CONTENTS
Lists all parts of your book and tells you where to find them

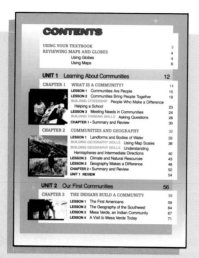

Your textbook contains many special features that will help you learn about communities.

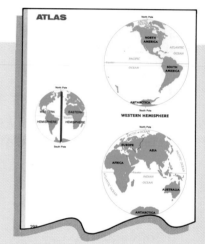

ATLAS

ATLAS
Maps of the United States and the world

REVIEWING MAPS & GLOBES

REVIEWING MAPS AND GLOBES
Reviews skills that will help you use the maps in your book

LESSON OPENER
Important vocabulary, people, and places introduced in the lesson

Lesson introduction

Asks you what you know from a lesson you have already read or from your own experience

Question you should think about as you read the lesson

LESSON
1 A New Country

READ TO LEARN

■ **Key Vocabulary**
American Revolution
Declaration of Independence

■ **Key People**
Thomas Jefferson

■ **Key Places**
Lexington, Massachusetts
Philadelphia, Pennsylvania

■ **Read Aloud**
A little over 200 years ago, our country was not a country at all. Parts of it were colonies ruled by governments in Europe. By 1750 England ruled 13 colonies along the coast near the Atlantic Ocean. But as the English colonies grew, so did the fights between England's leaders and the colonists.

This handmade blanket shows what a community in the American colonies looked like.

■ **Read for Purpose**
1. **WHAT YOU KNOW:** Name two communities in North America that began as colonies.
2. **WHAT YOU WILL LEARN:** Why did the English colonies decide to break away from England?

251

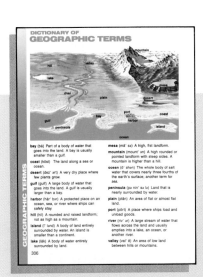

DICTIONARY OF GEOGRAPHIC TERMS

Defines and pronounces important geography terms

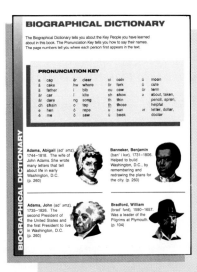

BIOGRAPHICAL DICTIONARY

Identifies and pronounces the names of important people discussed in your book and gives the page where each is introduced

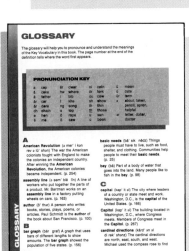

GLOSSARY

Defines and pronounces all Key Vocabulary and gives the page where each is introduced

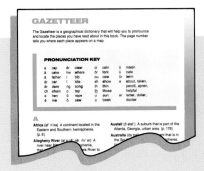

GAZETTEER

Identifies and pronounces important places discussed in your book and gives the page where each is shown on a map

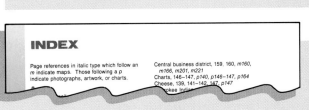

INDEX

Lists in alphabetical order people, places, events, and subjects in your book and gives the pages where they are found

Using Globes

Key Vocabulary
North Pole
South Pole
equator

Most of us
will never travel
throughout the
whole world. But
we can learn many
things about the world
by using maps and globes.
Maps and globes can help us
to "see the world" without leaving home.

Look at the picture of the earth shown above. The
picture was taken from far out in space. The white
shapes in the picture are clouds. Beneath the clouds you
can see land and water.

Looking at a globe is like looking at the earth from
space. A globe is a model, or small copy, of the earth.
Look at the picture of the globe on the next page. It
shows the same part of the earth that is shown in the
picture.

4

The Poles and Equator

Find the North Pole and the South Pole on the globe on this page. The North Pole is the place farthest north on the earth. The South Pole is the place farthest south. The North Pole and the South Pole are opposite each other.

There is an imaginary line halfway between the North and South poles that goes completely around the earth. This line is called the equator (i kwā′ tər). It divides the earth into a northern half and a southern half. On a globe, the equator is shown as a real line. Find the equator on the globe.

1. What is a globe?
2. What is the equator?
3. Why are globes so useful?

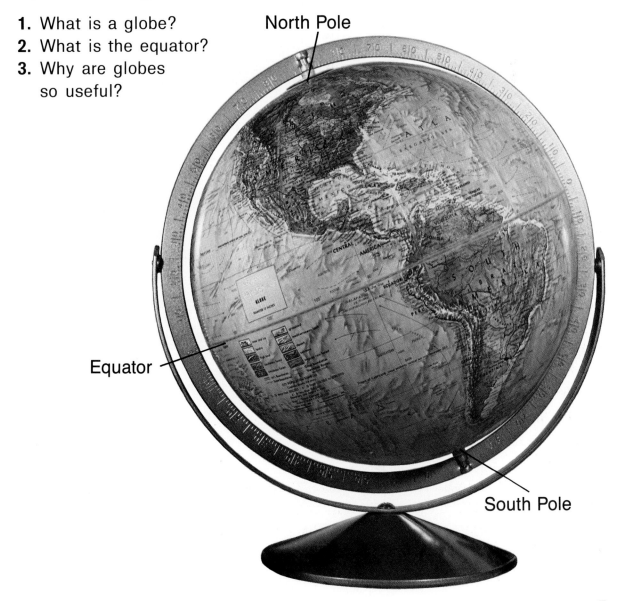

North Pole

Equator

South Pole

Using Maps

Key Vocabulary

continent   cardinal directions   symbol

ocean   compass rose   map key

     A map is a flat drawing of the earth or part of the
earth. Even though globes are really a better way of
showing the earth, maps are very useful. Maps can be
printed in books, which are easy to carry. Also, a map
can show you the whole world at one time. On a globe
you can only see half the world at one time.

     Most maps have titles. The title usually tells what
part of the world is shown on the map. It may also tell
you what kind of information the map gives. What is the
title of the map on this page?

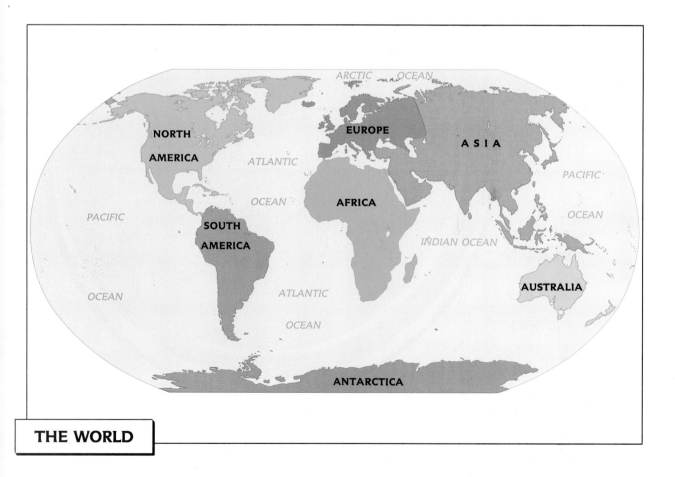

THE WORLD

Continents and Oceans

The earth has seven continents. A continent is a very large body of land. Name the continents shown on the world map on page 6. The earth also has four very large bodies of water called oceans. The oceans are also shown on the world map. What are their names?

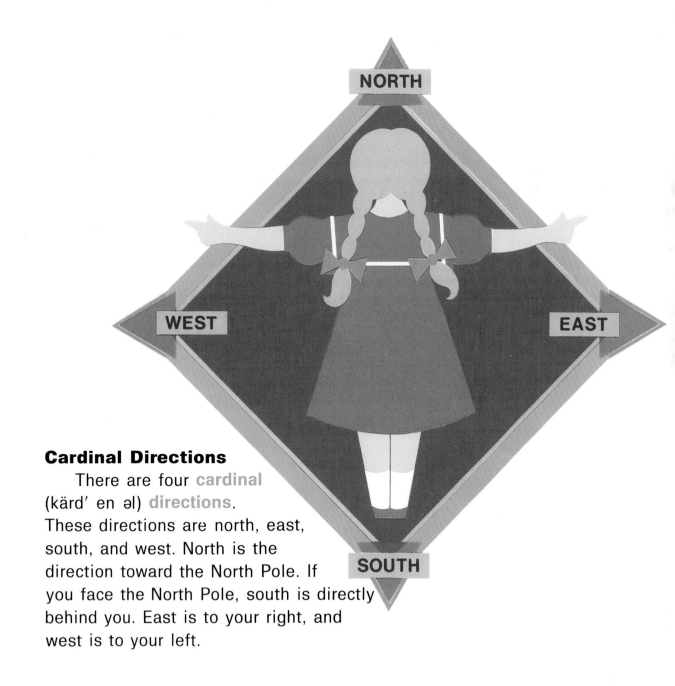

Cardinal Directions

There are four cardinal (kärd′ en əl) directions. These directions are north, east, south, and west. North is the direction toward the North Pole. If you face the North Pole, south is directly behind you. East is to your right, and west is to your left.

Compass Rose

Not all maps show the North Pole. How do you find directions without knowing where the North Pole is? A compass rose can help you. A compass rose, like a compass, can help you find directions. Look at the picture of a compass below. The needle of a compass will show you where north is.

Now look at the compass rose below. Letters are used to show the cardinal directions. North is shown by **N**, east by **E**, south by **S**, and west by **W**.

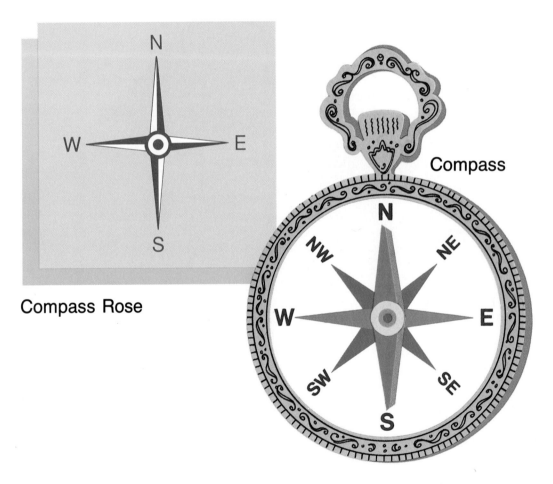

Compass

Compass Rose

Look at the map on the next page. It is a map of the continent of North America. Find the compass rose on the map. What country is south of the United States? What country is north of the United States? Name the ocean that is east of the United States.

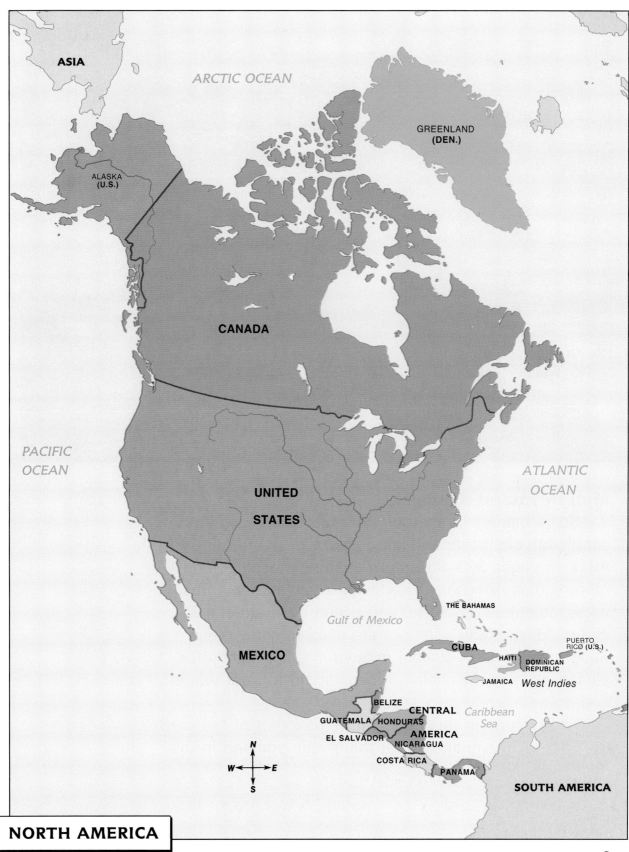

ASIA

ARCTIC OCEAN

GREENLAND
(DEN.)

ALASKA
(U.S.)

CANADA

*PACIFIC
OCEAN*

*ATLANTIC
OCEAN*

UNITED

STATES

Gulf of Mexico

THE BAHAMAS

MEXICO

CUBA

PUERTO
RICO (U.S.)

HAITI

DOMINICAN
REPUBLIC

JAMAICA

West Indies

BELIZE

CENTRAL

*Caribbean
Sea*

GUATEMALA

HONDURAS

AMERICA

EL SALVADOR

NICARAGUA

N

COSTA RICA

W — E

PANAMA

S

SOUTH AMERICA

NORTH AMERICA

Map Keys and Symbols

Some maps, like the one on page 6, show only continents and oceans. Some maps, like the one in the Atlas on pages 300–301, show countries, oceans, and other bodies of water. Other maps show states, cities, lakes, mountains, deserts, parks, and even streets and buildings. Map symbols are used to show these things on a map. A symbol is anything that stands for something else. Symbols on maps stand for real things and real places.

The picture on this page shows how part of the earth looks from an airplane. What things can you see in the picture?

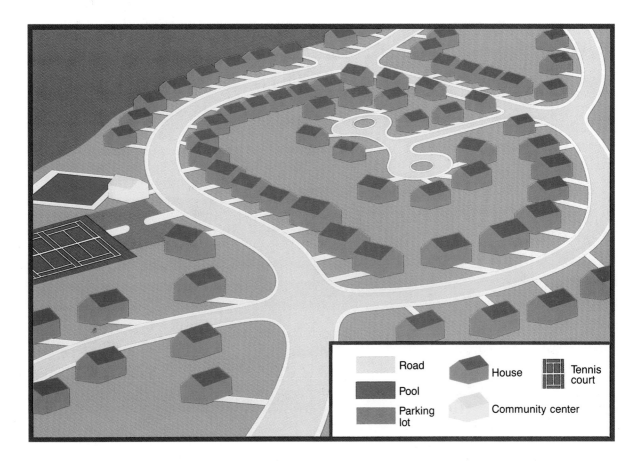

	Road		House		Tennis court
	Pool				
	Parking lot		Community center		

Now look at a map of the same area that is shown in the picture. The places in the picture are shown as symbols on the map. To understand the symbols, read the map key. The map key explains what each symbol means.

Some of the symbols used on the map are colors. What color is used for roads? Other symbols used on the map are small drawings that look like the things for which they stand. What does the symbol stand for? Find the symbol for a tennis court. How many tennis courts are shown on the map?

1. What is a map?
2. Why is a compass rose useful?
3. How do map keys help us to use maps?
4. Why are maps so useful?

UNIT 1

LEARNING ABOUT COMMUNITIES

WHERE WE ARE

Communities are found in many different places. Some are near rivers or oceans. Others are near mountains or forests. You can see some of these places on this map of our country. In this unit you will learn what communities are. You will also learn about the places where communities are found.

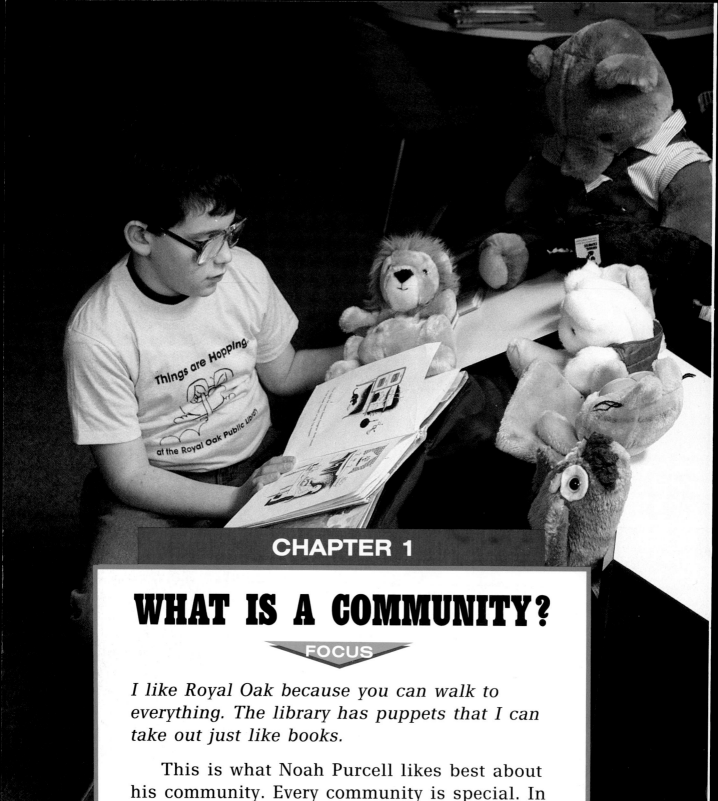

CHAPTER 1

WHAT IS A COMMUNITY?

▼ FOCUS

I like Royal Oak because you can walk to everything. The library has puppets that I can take out just like books.

This is what Noah Purcell likes best about his community. Every community is special. In this chapter you will learn how communities are alike. You will read more about Noah and his community in Lesson 3.

1 Communities Are People

READ TO LEARN

■ Key Vocabulary

community

■ Read Aloud

On their way to school one day, Susan Owens and Matthew Townes see a strange sign. Look at the sign in the picture on this page.

Riverdale is the place where Susan and Matthew live. They wonder what the sign means. How is Riverdale going to send a message to the future?

At school, Susan and Matthew's teacher tells the class about the sign. She explains that the leaders of Riverdale want to put a special box in the ground. The box will be a time capsule. It will be full of things that will tell people hundreds of years from now what Riverdale was like.

This is the sign Susan and Matthew saw. What does it say?

■ Read for Purpose

1. **WHAT YOU KNOW**: What is the name of the place where you live?
2. **WHAT YOU WILL LEARN**: What is a community?

15

What will the time capsule tell people in the future about Riverdale?

UNDERSTANDING A COMMUNITY

Susan and Matthew's teacher tells them that the time capsule should show that Riverdale is a community (kə mū′ nə tē). A community is a group of people working together, and the places where they live, work, have fun, and share special times. Suppose your community was making a time capsule. What would you put in it?

Look at the picture on this page. It shows the things Matthew chooses to put in the time capsule. Matthew wants a map of Riverdale and a telephone book.

Matthew explains, "The telephone book will show that we have homes, schools, libraries, and places for people to shop. A map will show where these places are."

Susan likes Matthew's ideas, but she wants to include some other things in the time capsule. She explains why. "Some important things about Riverdale," she says, "are not in a telephone book or on a map. People in a community also do special things together."

To show some of the special things people share in Riverdale, Susan adds a baseball cap. It will show that Riverdale has sports teams for children. She also adds a balloon.

Look at the writing on the balloon in the picture. What does it say? Every spring Riverdale has a big fair. Everyone in Riverdale has fun at the fair.

COMMUNITIES ARE ALIKE

How is your community like Susan and Matthew's community? All communities are like Riverdale in some ways. All communities are made up of people. Like Riverdale, they have homes for people to live in and stores where people shop. There are schools and places where people go to pray. There are places where people go to have fun.

What else could they put in the time capsule to tell people about their **community**?

17

Many communities have parks that all the people in the community share.

Many places are shared by all the people in the community. Think of all the things you share with the people in your community. You share the same roads and parks. You share schools and libraries, too.

This year you will learn many things about communities. You will see how communities are alike. You will also learn that communities can be very different.

 Check Your Reading

1. Explain what a community is.
2. How are communities alike?
3. **THINKING SKILL**: What places do people in your community share?

READ TO LEARN

Key Vocabulary

custom

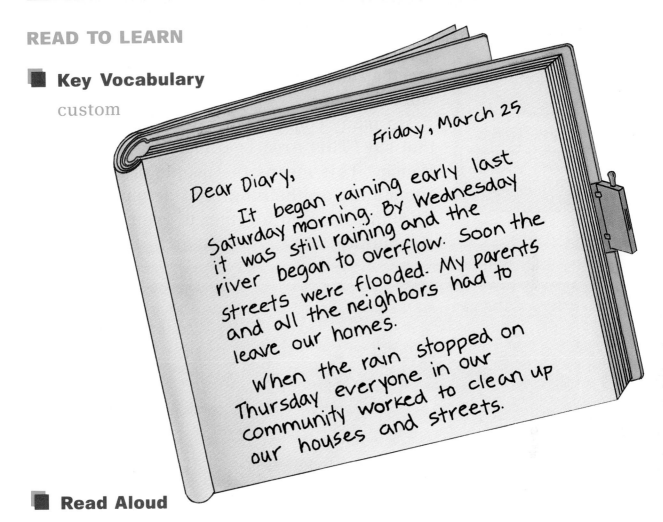

Friday, March 25

Dear Diary,

It began raining early last Saturday morning. By Wednesday it was still raining and the river began to overflow. Soon the streets were flooded. My parents and all the neighbors had to leave our homes.

When the rain stopped on Thursday everyone in our community worked to clean up our houses and streets.

Read Aloud

This is how Alison Fox described a flood in her community. People in communities often work together when there are problems. They also come together to share happy times.

Read for Purpose

1. **WHAT YOU KNOW**: How do the people in your community work together?
2. **WHAT YOU WILL LEARN**: How do customs bring people together?

19

WORKING TOGETHER

People in a community care about each other. This is why they work together to solve problems, as the people in Alison's community did. Many people working together can do more than one person working alone.

In many communities, there are signs that say "This Area Is Under Neighborhood Watch." This means the people of the community are helping their neighbors. They are working together to keep their community safe.

These people are piling up sandbags to keep a river from flooding their community.

SHARING CUSTOMS

People in communities also join together to share holidays and customs (kus' təmz). A custom is the special way a group of people does things. Having turkey on Thanksgiving is one example of a custom.

Some customs are shared by all the people in one community. Remember the fair in Susan and Matthew's community that you read about in Lesson 1? The fair is a custom shared by all the people in Riverdale.

Some holidays and customs are shared by all the communities in our country. On the Fourth of July, communities celebrate our country's birthday. Does your community have any special Fourth of July customs?

It is a custom in many communities to have picnics, parades, or fireworks on this holiday. People may sing the song on the next page. It is called "America." Look at the words. The words make us feel proud of our country.

Communities celebrate the Fourth of July with parades and fireworks.

AMERICA

Music by Henry Carey
Words by Samuel F. Smith

Moderato

My coun - try, 'tis of thee, Sweet land of
lib - er - ty, Of thee I sing;
Land where my fath - ers died, Land of the Pil - grim's pride,
From ev - 'ry __ moun - tain - side Let __ free - dom ring.

Check Your Reading

1. Why do people in communities work together?
2. Name two Fourth of July customs.
3. **THINKING SKILL**: What customs do people share in your community?

22

HELPING A SCHOOL

Joe Medalia (mə dāl′ yə) owns a company called Medalia Salvage. A salvage company buys old machines and other things made of metal. These things are taken apart, and the parts are then reused. Joe uses his salvage business in a special way to help his community. He uses it to help a whole school.

Medalia Salvage is located in the community of Seattle, Washington. The company works together with students at the Wilson-Pacific School. This school helps young people with learning disabilities or handicaps to get ready for jobs. Joe Medalia wants to help the students.

One way Joe helps the students is by finding materials for classes at the school. He gave one class a huge computer. The class learned how to take the computer apart. Then they reused some pieces, and sold the rest. The students earned money for their school while they were learning.

Two classes meet at Medalia Salvage each day. There the students learn how to take apart typewriters and other office machines.

The school also needed to find some beginning jobs for the students. Joe talked to people who owned businesses in the community. He found other people, like himself, who were glad to hire the students.

Both Joe and the school are happy with their partnership. Joe thinks that the happiness he gets from his friendships with the students is a fair trade for all his time and work.

3 Meeting Needs in Communities

After doing everything on his Saturday list, Noah likes to play basketball.

READ TO LEARN

Key Vocabulary

basic needs
goods
services

Read Aloud

Noah Purcell lives in the community of Royal Oak, Michigan. On Friday everyone in his family makes a list of things to do on Saturday. Have you ever made a list? Many people make lists to help them remember things they need to do.

The lists Noah's family made are shown on the next page. They show some things his family needs. They also show the places they will go in their community to meet these needs. People in the community of Royal Oak help Noah's family meet their needs.

Read for Purpose

1. **WHAT YOU KNOW**: Make a list of things you might do on Saturday. How is your list the same as Noah's? How is it different?

2. **WHAT YOU WILL LEARN**: How do communities help people meet their needs?

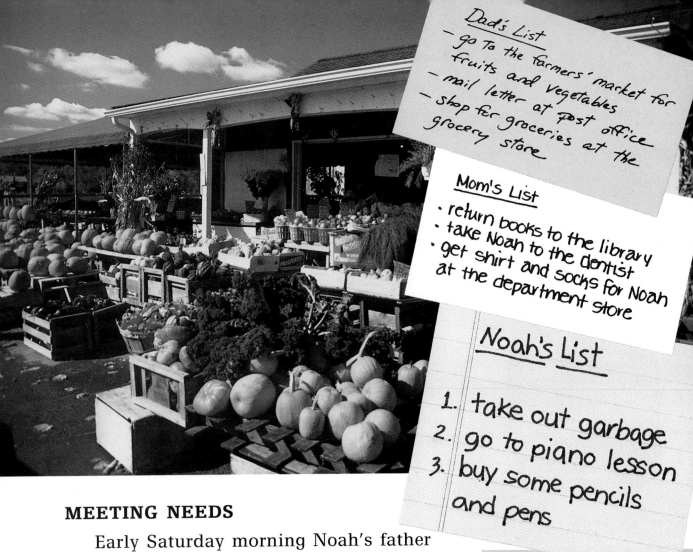

Dad's List
- go to the farmers' market for fruits and vegetables
- mail letter at post office
- shop for groceries at the grocery store

Mom's List
- return books to the library
- take Noah to the dentist
- get shirt and socks for Noah at the department store

Noah's List
1. take out garbage
2. go to piano lesson
3. buy some pencils and pens

MEETING NEEDS

Early Saturday morning Noah's father drives to the farmers' market. Most food sold at the market is grown nearby. Food is one of our **basic needs**. Basic needs are things people must have to live. All people must have food to eat to make them strong and healthy. Shelter and clothing are other basic needs.

Few people today grow their own food, build their own houses, or make all their own clothes. People depend on other people in their community to help them meet their basic needs. Look again at the lists. What things on their lists will help Noah's family meet their needs?

Which person in Noah's family is going to the farmers' market? What **basic need** will be met by going there?

25

GOODS AND SERVICES

Needs are met in different ways. One way communities help people meet their needs is by having places where people can buy goods. Goods are things that people make or grow. Fruits, books, and toys are all goods. So are the clothes you are wearing and the notebook you use in school.

Communities also help people meet their needs by providing services. A service is work that helps other people. Your teacher and doctor provide services. The people who work in grocery stores and department stores also provide services.

Noah forgot to put his trip to the dentist on his Saturday list. His mother remembered it. He did put his piano lesson on his list. Noah's dentist and piano teacher both provide services.

Groceries are one example of goods. When Noah and his mother buy shirts in a department store, they are also buying goods.

26

COMMUNITY SERVICES ARE FOR EVERYONE

Look at the lists again. There are several things on the lists that we have not yet mentioned. Noah has to take out the garbage. Noah's mother will return books to the librarian at the public library.

The sanitation workers who pick up the garbage and the librarian who sorts the books are community workers. They provide services for everyone in Royal Oak. What other important community workers can you name? Do not forget firefighters and police officers. They make Royal Oak safe. Why are letter carriers important in a community?

Firefighters and letter carriers provide **services** to everyone in a community.

✔ Check Your Reading

1. Name two basic needs.
2. What is the difference between goods and services?
3. **THINKING SKILL**: Make two lists. On one list write five goods sold in your community. On the other list write five services provided in your community.

27

Asking Questions

Asking questions is one way to learn things you want to know. To ask a good question you need to think about what it is you want to know.

If you wanted to learn your friend's address, one good question to ask is "What street do you live on?" You would not ask, "What color is your house?"

Trying the Skill

Matthew is helping Mr. Costa sell popcorn at the Riverdale Fair. Mr. Costa has given him the following information.

I will pop the corn and put it in this large bowl. You can scoop it into some bags. Put the money you collect for the popcorn in this box.

1. What other information does Matthew need to know?
2. What questions will give him the other information?

POPCORN

HELPING YOURSELF

One Way to Ask Good Questions	Example
1. Choose something you would like to learn more about.	You want to know more about selling popcorn.
2. Ask yourself, "What information do I need to know?"	What do you need to know in order to sell popcorn?
3. List the questions you can ask to get the information. You can use question starters such as *who*, *what*, *when*, and *how* to write your questions.	One question you might ask is, "How much does a bag of popcorn cost?"

Applying the Skill

Read the story about a custom in Kim's community.

Kim and her family have just moved to a new community. In school, everyone is making plans to go to the Apple Festival. Kim wants to know more about this community custom.

Read the following questions. Choose the best answer.

1. What should Kim do first?
   a. ask questions
   b. think about what she wants to know
   c. go to the Apple Festival

2. What question or questions should Kim ask?
   a. Where and when is the festival?
   b. What do you do at the festival?
   c. both a and b

Reviewing the Skill

1. What is one way you can follow to ask good questions?
2. What are two questions you could ask to find out more about the Riverdale Fair?
3. Give three examples of words that are good question starters.
4. Why is it important to be able to ask good questions?

IDEAS TO REMEMBER

- A community is a group of people who work together, and the places where they live, work, have fun, and share special times.
- Sharing customs brings together people in communities.
- Communities help people to meet their needs by providing goods and services.

REVIEWING VOCABULARY

basic needs   goods

community   services

custom

Number a sheet of paper from 1 to 5. Beside each number write the word or term from the list above that best completes each sentence.

1. Going to a parade on Memorial Day is one example of a _____.
2. Jeremy goes to the store to buy pencils, a notebook, and other _____.
3. A mail carrier provides _____ to the community.
4. Food, clothing, and shelter are examples of _____.
5. People in a _____ live, work, and share special times together.

REVIEWING FACTS

1. Name five places found in all communities.
2. Why were the people of Riverdale making a time capsule?
3. What are some ways people in a community share customs?
4. Tell whether each item in this list is a *good* or a *service*.
   a. potatoes
   b. television
   c. teaching school
   d. bus driving
   e. fire fighting
5. List three ways in which people in a community help meet each other's needs.

WRITING ABOUT MAIN IDEAS

1. **Writing a Letter:** Write a letter to Susan Owens. Tell her what you would put in a time

capsule for your community and explain why.

2. **Writing a Paragraph:** Look at the photo on page 20. Write a paragraph telling how people in a community work together.

3. **Making a List:** Make a list of four stores in your community. Beside each one write a sentence telling what goods or services each store provides.

BUILDING SKILLS: ASKING QUESTIONS

Read the following paragraph. Then answer the questions that follow it.

Austin wants to march in his community's Fourth of July parade. He knows the parade always takes place on July 4. Many people in Austin's community join in the parade each year.

1. What are some steps you can use to ask good questions?

2. What are two questions Austin can ask to find out more about the parade?

3. Why is it important to be able to ask good questions?

STUDYING YOUR COMMUNITY

In Chapter 1 you read about communities. Your local newspaper tells a lot about things going on in your community. Read the newspaper every day for a week. With your parents' permission, cut out articles about people working together to help your community. Also cut out articles about special events or local customs. Then arrange the articles in a scrapbook. Write a sentence to go with each article.

CHAPTER 2

COMMUNITIES AND GEOGRAPHY

FOCUS

*O, there's wild raging oceans and proud mountain
  chains,*
Green peaceful valleys and wide grassy plains. . . .
                        from "Little Blue Top" by Tony Hughes

These words are part of a song about the
earth. In this chapter you will read about the
land and its features. You will see how
communities are special because of the land
and water around them.

1 Landforms and Bodies of Water

READ TO LEARN

■ Key Vocabulary

landform
plain

■ Key Places

Mississippi River
Rocky Mountains

■ Read Aloud

One way to learn about the land we live on is to read the stories people tell about the land. Many of these stories are "tall tales." In a tall tale the truth is stretched to make the story fun to tell. Another way to learn about the land is to study its features. Mountains, hills, and rivers are some of these important features.

In this lesson you are going to learn about the land both ways. First you will read a tall tale. Then you will learn more about real places like rivers, lakes, and mountains.

■ Read for Purpose

1. **WHAT YOU KNOW**: Is your community located near any mountains, lakes, or rivers?

2. **WHAT YOU WILL LEARN**: What is a landform?

A river is one kind of feature of the land we live on.

33

A TALL TALE ABOUT
Paul Bunyan

Paul Bunyan was so big that everything he did had huge results. Even a little mistake caused huge problems. There was the time on a cold winter day that he almost caused a terrible flood. He spilled a huge tank of water that he was carrying back from the Great Lakes.

Paul spilled so much water that many homes and farms were in danger of being washed away. So he grabbed a shovel and started to dig a huge ditch to hold the water. He dug the ditch all the way to the Gulf of Mexico.

As Paul dug, he threw the dirt from the ditch to the west. People say that this ditch became the Mississippi River. They say that the dirt made the Rocky Mountains.

REAL PLACES

Do you see why the Paul Bunyan story is called a "tall tale"? The things it describes did not really happen. But the places it tells about are real.

Look at the map of the United States below. You can find the places described in the Paul Bunyan tale on this map. Find the Rocky Mountains, the Great Lakes, the Mississippi River, and the Gulf of Mexico. Let's find out more about these places, and places like them.

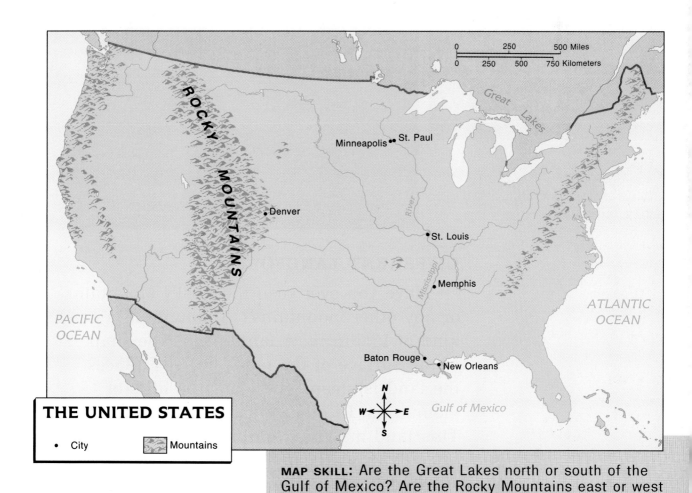

THE UNITED STATES

- City

Mountains

MAP SKILL: Are the Great Lakes north or south of the Gulf of Mexico? Are the Rocky Mountains east or west of the Mississippi River?

Plains, hills, and mountains are all **landforms**. How are they different?

DIFFERENT LANDFORMS

Have you ever seen the Rocky Mountains or any other mountains? A mountain is one kind of landform. A landform is the shape of the surface of the land. In some places the land is steep. There may be hills or mountains. In other places the land is flat. This land may be a plain. Flat, grassy land is called a plain.

Find the Dictionary of Geographic Terms on page 306. Landforms such as mountains and plains are described there.

DIFFERENT BODIES OF WATER

The Mississippi River and the Great Lakes are mentioned in the Paul Bunyan tale. Bodies of water such as rivers and lakes are also described in the Dictionary of Geographic Terms. How is a river different from a lake?

The largest bodies of water on the earth are oceans. Look at the map on pages 300–301 of the Atlas. Name the four oceans shown on this map. Oceans cover more of our earth than land does. You can see this for yourself by looking at a globe.

STUDYING OUR LAND

Landforms and bodies of water are just two things we study to learn about the land we live on. Plants, animals, and the weather are also important. You will learn more about them in the next lesson.

Check Your Reading

1. Explain what a landform is.
2. Name two types of landforms and two types of bodies of water.
3. GEOGRAPHY SKILL: Name all the bodies of water shown on the map on page 35.
4. THINKING SKILL: Describe a landform or body of water located near your community.

This winding river is located in the state of Colorado.

Using Map Scales

Key Vocabulary

scale

Even a person as big as Paul Bunyan would be too small to use a map that showed the real size of places. Maps have to be much smaller than the places they show. The scale (skāl) of a map helps to show you the real size of places. It helps you to find the real distance between places.

Reading a Scale

Look at the scale on **Map A** on page 39. The scale tells you how many miles on the earth are shown by one inch on the map. It also tells how many kilometers are shown by two centimeters. How many miles does one inch show? How many kilometers do two centimeters show?

To use the scale, you will need a strip of paper. Look at the scale below. Slide the top edge of your paper along the line for miles and mark it as shown below. Then do the same for kilometers.

Now use the scale you have made to find the distance across Colorado from west to east on **Map A**. Place the strip of paper along either the northern or southern border of Colorado. Place the **0** on the western border. Then, read the number that is closest to the eastern border. You will see that the distance across Colorado is about 400 miles. About how many kilometers is it across Colorado?

Different Scales

Not all maps have the same scale. The scale on **Map B** on page 39 is different from the scale on **Map A**. Does an inch on **Map B** show a larger or smaller distance than an inch on **Map A**?

Maps have different scales because maps show larger or

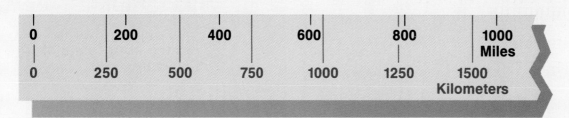

0	200	400	600	800	1000 Miles
0	250	500	750	1000	1250	1500 Kilometers

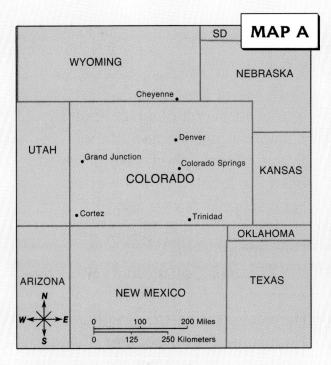

MAP A

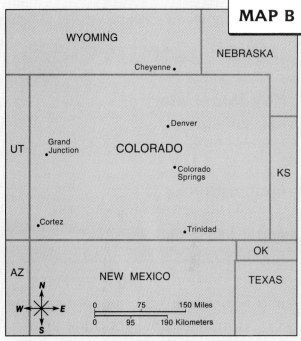

MAP B

smaller parts of the earth. Distances on the earth always remain the same. You can check this by finding the east–west distance across Colorado on **Map B**. Use a strip of paper to make a new scale. Then use it to measure as you did before. You will find that the real distance across Colorado is still about 400 miles, or 625 kilometers.

Suppose you want to find the distance between the communities of Cortez and Trinidad. Place your scale for **Map B** with the edge just below the dots for the two communities. Place the **0** by the dot for Cortez. Then read the mark on your scale that appears next to Trinidad. Cortez is 225 miles, or 400 kilometers, from Trinidad.

Reviewing the Skill

1. What is a map scale?
2. How many miles is it across Colorado from north to south?
3. How many kilometers is it from Cortez to Grand Junction?
4. Why is it important to be able to read map scales?

Understanding Hemispheres and Intermediate Directions

Key Vocabulary

hemisphere

intermediate directions

Hemispheres

You already know that the earth, like a ball, is round. Another name for a round body is a sphere (sfêr). A ball, the earth, and a globe are all spheres.

No matter how you look at a sphere, you can see only half of it at a time. You can check this by looking at a globe. Half a sphere is called a **hemisphere** (hem' is sfêr). *Hemi* means "half."

The maps on the next page will help you to understand how the earth is divided into hemispheres. Each map shows one half of the earth.

The maps at the top of the page show the Western Hemisphere and the Eastern Hemisphere. The Eastern Hemisphere and the Western Hemisphere are opposite halves of the earth. All of which four continents are located in the Eastern Hemisphere? All of which ocean is located in the Eastern Hemisphere? Name two continents located in the Western Hemisphere.

The maps at the bottom of the page show the Northern Hemisphere and the Southern Hemisphere. The equator divides the Northern Hemisphere from the Southern Hemisphere. The Northern Hemisphere is the half you would see if you looked at the earth from directly above the North Pole. The Southern Hemisphere is the half you would see if you looked at the earth from directly above the South Pole.

Look again at the maps at the bottom of the next page. In what hemisphere is the continent of Antarctica located? In what hemisphere is the Arctic Ocean located?

WESTERN HEMISPHERE

EASTERN HEMISPHERE

NORTHERN HEMISPHERE

SOUTHERN HEMISPHERE

Directions

You have already learned that you can use a compass rose to help you find directions on a map. Look at the compass rose on the map on this page. The compass rose uses letters for cardinal directions. North is shown by **N**, east by **E**, south by **S**, and west by **W**.

A compass rose can also be used to find in-between or intermediate directions. Intermediate directions are halfway between the cardinal directions. The intermediate directions are northeast,

southeast, southwest, and northwest. Look at the compass rose on this page. What intermediate direction is between North and West?

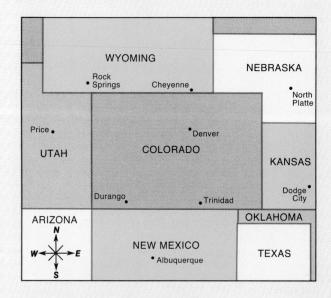

Reviewing the Skill

Use the hemisphere maps on page 41 and the map and compass rose on this page to answer these questions.
1. What are intermediate directions?
2. All of which continent is in both the Western Hemisphere and the Northern Hemisphere?
3. In what direction is Denver from Durango?
4. Why is it important to know intermediate directions?

COMPASS ROSE

NORTH
N

Northwest   Northeast
NW   NE

WEST W   E EAST

SW   SE
Southwest   Southeast

S
SOUTH

▬ Cardinal direction
▬ Intermediate direction

2 Climate and Natural Resources

READ TO LEARN

Key Vocabulary
climate
natural resource
geography

Key Places
Juneau, Alaska
Honolulu, Hawaii

Read Aloud

In the last lesson you read about the many different landforms and bodies of water in the United States. Our country also has many different plants and animals. Some parts of the United States are covered with forests. Other parts are grasslands. There are alligators in Florida, and moose in Maine.

The weather is also different in different parts of our country. For example, the weather in the North is colder than the weather in the South.

Knowing about the plants, animals, and weather of a place is important to understanding the land we live on.

Alligators live in the southern part of our country.

Read for Purpose

1. **WHAT YOU KNOW**: What kinds of plants and animals are found near your community?
2. **WHAT YOU WILL LEARN**: What is geography?

Juneau, Alaska, (*left*) and Honolulu, Hawaii, (*right*) have very different climates.

WEATHER AND CLIMATE

Weather is the way it is outdoors each day. Is it hot and rainy? Is it cold and dry? The weather may change from one day to the next. Climate (klī′ mit) is the kind of weather a place has over a long time. Communities in different places have different climates.

What kind of climate does your community have? Juneau (jü′ nō), Alaska, is located in the North. Juneau has very short summers and long, snowy winters. Honolulu, Hawaii, is in the South. Honolulu has a climate that is warm all year long.

44

NATURAL RESOURCES

Climate is one reason places in our country are so different. Natural resources (nach′ ər əl rē′ sôrs iz) are another reason our land is different. A natural resource is something found in nature that people use. Trees, water, animals, and soil are all examples of natural resources. A good climate is also a natural resource.

How do people use natural resources? People use them to make food and other goods. For example, soil and water are used to grow food. Trees are used to make goods such as furniture and paper.

(*above*) Paper is made from trees, which are an important natural resource. (*below*) *Workers check the growth of trees in a forest.*

PROTECTING NATURAL RESOURCES

Natural resources must be used carefully so we do not run out of them. Everyone can learn to use natural resources wisely. You can save resources by not wasting water or paper.

Often people in a community can work together to protect resources. For example, they can make sure a river or a lake is kept clean. Can you think of any other ways people in a community can work together to protect resources?

Old newspapers can be reused to make new paper. Reusing paper helps protect our natural resources.

BE A TREE SAVER

GEOGRAPHY

When you study the land where you live, you are studying geography (jē og′ rə fē). Geography is the study of the landforms, bodies of water, climate, and natural resources of a place. People and their activities are also part of geography. Sometimes people change geography.

In the next lesson you will see how geography makes a difference to communities.

People used machines to build the dam shown here. This is one way people change geography.

Check Your Reading

1. What are two things that make the land in our country different?
2. Name three kinds of natural resources.
3. **GEOGRAPHY SKILL**: What is geography?
4. **THINKING SKILL**: Describe the geography of your community.

3 Geography Makes a Difference

READ TO LEARN

Key Places

Memphis, Tennessee
Pompano Beach, Florida
Fancy Prairie, Illinois

Read Aloud

Studying geography is a little like doing a puzzle. You can think of landforms, bodies of water, climate, and natural resources as the pieces of the puzzle. You can put these puzzle pieces of information together and find out many things about communities.

Geography can help you understand why people first came to a place, or why a community grew slowly or quickly. The puzzle pieces fit together to make a picture of a community. The information shows you how geography makes a difference to communities.

Read for Purpose

1. **WHAT YOU KNOW**: Is your community growing slowly or quickly?

    2. **WHAT YOU WILL LEARN**: How does geography make a difference to communities?

LANDFORMS AND WATER MAKE A DIFFERENCE

You read about the Mississippi River in Lesson 1. Find the Mississippi River on the map in your Atlas on pages 302–303. Now use your finger to follow the path of the Mississippi River. Follow the river from its beginning in the north until it empties into the Gulf of Mexico. Notice how many names of communities your finger touches.

People started building communities along the Mississippi River long ago. At that time traveling by boat was the fastest way to get from place to place. Find Memphis, Tennessee, on the map. This community began as a place where boats picked up and dropped off goods.

Now find the Rocky Mountains in the Atlas on pages 304–305. The Rocky Mountains are very high mountains. Notice how few communities are shown on the map here. In very high mountains, there are usually only a few small communities. Why do you think this is so?

Boats carry goods to and from communities along the Mississippi River.

CLIMATE AND NATURAL RESOURCES MAKE A DIFFERENCE

Climate and natural resources can make a difference in the kinds of work people do and the ways they have fun. Pompano Beach, Florida, has a warm and sunny climate. Many older people choose to live here after they retire, or stop working, because of its good climate. Many people in Pompano Beach work to provide services for the retired people in this community.

In the town of Fancy Prairie, Illinois, many people are farmers. The good soil near this town is an important natural resource. It makes a difference in the kind of work people do. How do the climate and natural resources in your community make a difference?

(*above*) Good soil is one natural resource needed to grow corn. (*below*) A sunny climate is another important resource.

MAKING CHOICES

Learning about the geography of a place helps people make choices. It helps people answer many questions about a place. For example, "Is this a good place for a farm?" "Will it be easy to travel to this place?" "If we go there for a vacation, can we swim and fish?" In the next unit you will see how geography affected communities long ago.

 Check Your Reading

1. Why are there many communities along the Mississippi River?
2. How did geography help the community of Memphis to grow?
3. **GEOGRAPHY SKILL**: How does the geography of Pompano Beach make a difference in this community?
4. **THINKING SKILL**: What are three questions you could ask to learn the most about the geography of a community?

IDEAS TO REMEMBER

- Studying landforms and bodies of water is one way to learn about the land we live on.
- Our country has many different natural resources and climates.
- Geography makes a difference in the way people work and have fun in communities.

REVIEWING VOCABULARY

climate   natural resource
geography   plain
landforms

Number a sheet of paper from 1 to 5. Beside each number write the word or term from the list that best completes the sentence.

1. A _____ is flat, grassy land.
2. _____ is the study of the landforms, natural resources, and climate of a place.
3. If you know the _____ of a place, you know if it is warm there in the winter.
4. Hills, mountains, and plains are _____.
5. A _____ is something found in nature that people use.

REVIEWING FACTS

1. What is a "tall tale"?
2. Name two things that are facts in the Paul Bunyan tall tale. Name two made-up things.
3. What are the largest bodies of water on the earth?
4. Use the map on page 35 to name three bodies of water.
5. What is a landform?
6. What is the difference between weather and climate?
7. Name one way in which people change geography.
8. Name three natural resources.
9. Why must natural resources be used wisely?
10. How does geography affect the kind of work people do in a place?

◖◖◗ WRITING ABOUT MAIN IDEAS

1. **Writing a Letter:** Imagine you have a pen pal in another state. Write him or her a letter telling about the landforms and bodies of water in your

area. Also tell your pen pal about the area's climate and natural resources.

2. **Writing a Tall Tale:** Make up a tall tale about how a landform or a body of water was first made.

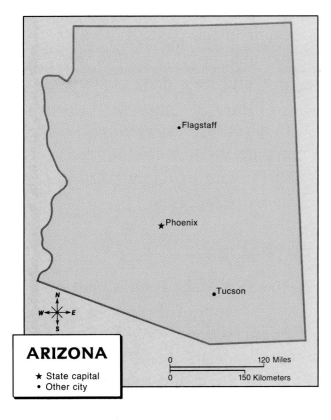

ARIZONA
★ State capital
• Other city

0   120 Miles

0   150 Kilometers

BUILDING SKILLS: USING MAP SCALES

Use the map and map scale above to answer these questions.

1. How many kilometers is Tucson from Phoenix? How many miles?

2. What is the distance across Arizona from east to west? What is the north-south distance across Arizona? Give your answers in both kilometers and miles.

3. Is Phoenix closer to Tucson or to Flagstaff?

4. Why is it important to know how to read a map scale?

STUDYING YOUR COMMUNITY

In Chapter 2 you read about landforms, bodies of water, and other features of geography. What is the geography like in your area? Use an atlas and books from the library to make a map of your state.

Use colors, labels, pictures, or symbols to show the following things on the map: the location of your community, the landforms in your state, the bodies of water in and near your state, and the natural resources found in your state. Be sure to include a map key explaining the colors and symbols you use.

REVIEWING VOCABULARY

basic needs	goods
climate	landform
community	natural resource
custom	plain
geography	services

Number a sheet of paper from 1 to 10. Beside each number write the word or term from the list above that matches the definition.

1. The weather over a long period of time
2. People and the places where they live, work, and share special times
3. Things that people make or grow
4. A shape of the surface of the land
5. Something found in nature that people can use
6. The special way a group of people does things
7. Work that helps other people
8. The study of the landforms, climate, natural resources, and effects of human activity on a place
9. Things people need to live
10. Flat, grassy land

✐ WRITING ABOUT THE UNIT

1. **Writing a Newspaper Story:** Think of a custom you would like to start in your community. It might be the celebration of a famous person's birthday or of an event in the past. Write a newspaper story telling why it would be a good custom.
2. **Writing a Paragraph:** Imagine that you are explaining geography to a first-grader. Write your explanation in a short paragraph.

ACTIVITIES

1. **Using a Map:** Find a map of your community. Locate your home, school, public library, and post office.
2. **Working Together to Make a Bulletin Board Display:** Everyone in the class should collect pictures that show some of the customs in your community. Write a sentence describing each picture. Use the pictures and sentences to make a bulletin board display.

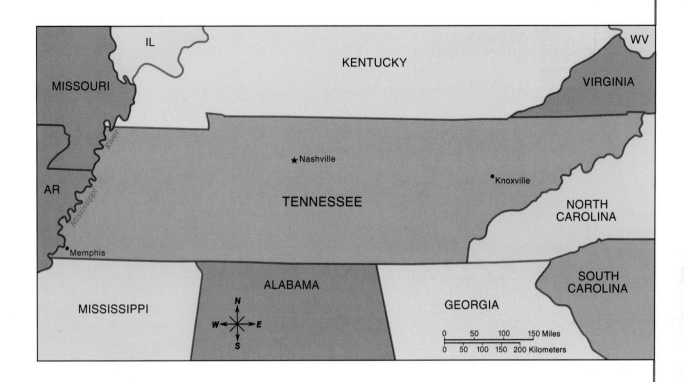

BUILDING SKILLS: UNDERSTANDING INTERMEDIATE DIRECTIONS

Use the map above to answer the following questions.

1. What are the intermediate directions?

2. What state is east of Tennessee?

3. What river forms the western border of Tennessee?

4. Why is it important to understand intermediate directions?

LINKING PAST, PRESENT, AND FUTURE

Interview an older person in your community. Ask the person how your community has changed over the years. Ask how the person thinks your community might change in the future. Then write a paragraph about what you have learned.

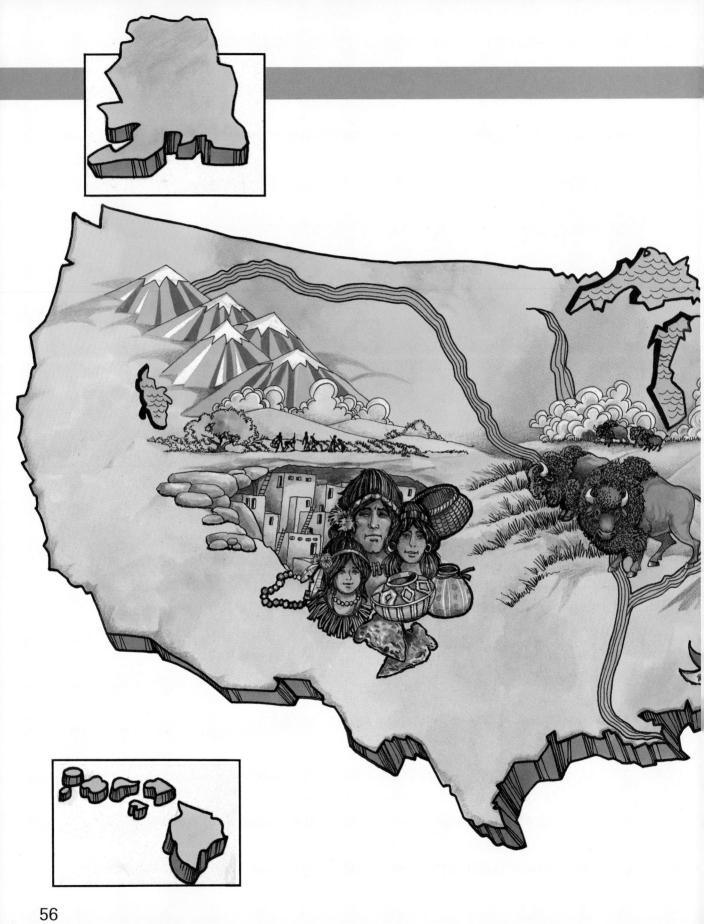

OUR FIRST COMMUNITIES

WHERE WE ARE

In this unit you will learn about three of our country's first communities. These communities were built by different groups of people. They were built in three very different places. Learning about them helps us to discover the story of our country's past.

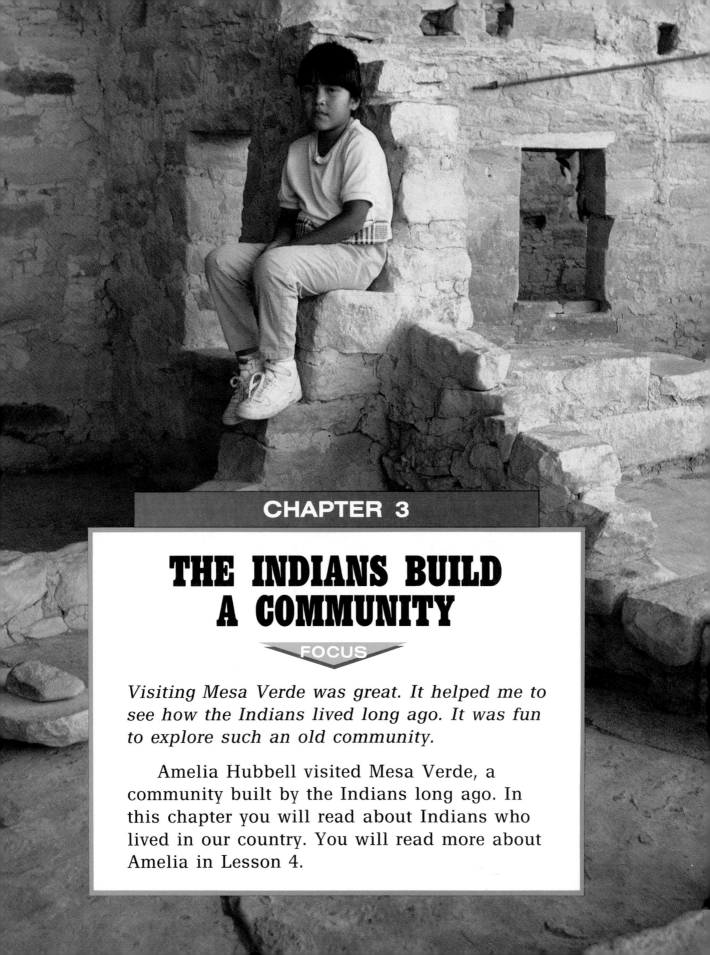

CHAPTER 3

THE INDIANS BUILD A COMMUNITY

FOCUS

Visiting Mesa Verde was great. It helped me to see how the Indians lived long ago. It was fun to explore such an old community.

Amelia Hubbell visited Mesa Verde, a community built by the Indians long ago. In this chapter you will read about Indians who lived in our country. You will read more about Amelia in Lesson 4.

1 The First Americans

READ TO LEARN

◼ Key Vocabulary

culture

◼ Read Aloud

Long ago North America was very different from the way it is today. There were no cities or highways. There were no schools or stores. But even long ago people lived in communities. They made their homes, food, and clothing from the plants and animals they found around them. The builders of these early communities were Indians—the first Americans.

Indians are also called Native Americans. A native is someone who was born in a place. The name Native American helps us remember that the Indians were the first people to live on the continent of North America.

◼ Read for Purpose

1. **WHAT YOU KNOW**: How do you think the first Americans met their basic needs?
2. **WHAT YOU WILL LEARN**: What is culture?

This doll and these shoes were made by Indians. The Indians were the first people to live in North America.

DIFFERENT CULTURES

Many different Indian groups lived in North America. Each group had its own language and customs. Several groups of Indians often shared the same culture (kul' chər). A culture is the way of life of a group of people. Every group of people has a culture. The language you speak, the clothes you wear, the food you eat, and the religion you believe in are all part of your culture.

Indian groups that shared the same culture had the same way of finding food and building houses. They depended on the same natural resources. They used these resources in the same way.

60

The map on this page shows some of the Indian groups that lived in the land that became the United States. The colors on the map tell you which groups shared the same culture. Each color stands for a different culture area. The pictures on the map show you some of the ways the people in each culture area lived. Find the Cherokee Indians on the map. They are part of the Eastern Woodlands culture area. Name the other groups that are part of this culture area.

MAP SKILL: Name the Indian culture areas shown on the map. What groups are part of the Plains culture?

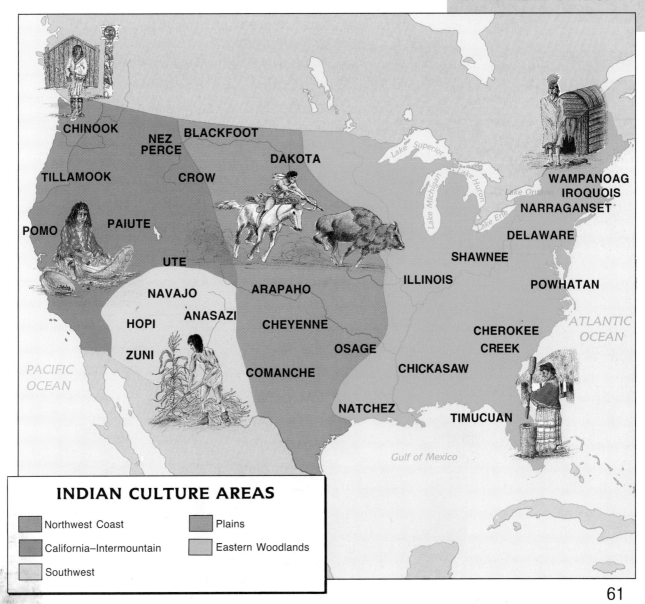

CHINOOK
NEZ PERCE
BLACKFOOT
DAKOTA
TILLAMOOK
CROW
POMO
PAIUTE
UTE
NAVAJO
ANASAZI
ARAPAHO
HOPI
CHEYENNE
ZUNI
OSAGE
COMANCHE
CHICKASAW
NATCHEZ
TIMUCUAN
WAMPANOAG
IROQUOIS
NARRAGANSET
DELAWARE
SHAWNEE
ILLINOIS
POWHATAN
CHEROKEE
CREEK

Lake Superior
Lake Michigan
Lake Huron
Lake Ontario
Lake Erie

ATLANTIC OCEAN
PACIFIC OCEAN
Gulf of Mexico

INDIAN CULTURE AREAS

- Northwest Coast
- California–Intermountain
- Southwest
- Plains
- Eastern Woodlands

THE CULTURE OF THE PLAINS INDIANS

Now find the Plains culture area on the map on page 61. These Indians lived in an area of our country known as the Great Plains. You can find the Great Plains in your Atlas on pages 304–305. Long ago huge herds of buffalo roamed the Great Plains. Here is how a visitor at that time described the buffalo.

> In every direction, as far as we could see, there were buffalo, buffalo, and still more buffalo. They were a grand sight.

Buffalo were an important resource of the Plains Indians. They used buffalo meat for food. They used buffalo skins to make clothing. The skins were even used to make their homes, called tepees. Tepees could be moved easily as the Indians followed the buffalo herds across the plains. Hunting buffalo was an important part of the culture of the Plains Indians.

Why was hunting buffalo such an important part of the culture of the Plains Indians?

CULTURE AND RESOURCES

Like the Plains Indians, the Indians in the other culture areas used the resources around them to meet their needs. But these resources were different.

Find the Southwest culture area on the map on page 61. These Indians were not hunters like the Plains Indians. There were no buffalo in the Southwest. Instead, they were farmers. Imagine how different life was for these Indians. In the next three lessons you will learn more about these Indians.

Plains Indian women made tepees from buffalo skins.

Check Your Reading

1. Why were buffalo important to the Plains Indians?

2. Name three things that are part of a group's culture.

3. **GEOGRAPHY SKILL**: What does the map on page 61 tell you about the culture of the Indians of the Southwest?

4. **THINKING SKILL**: In what ways might Indians who lived near your community long ago have met their needs?

2 The Geography of the Southwest

READ TO LEARN

■ **Key Vocabulary**
desert
mesa

■ **Key Places**
Mesa Verde

■ **Read Aloud**

The map on page 61 shows the area where the Anasazi (än ə säz′ ē) Indians once lived. These Indians were one of the groups of the Southwest culture. Like the Plains Indians you read about in Lesson 1, the Anasazi depended on the natural resources around them. The geography of the Southwest is very different from the Great Plains. This means that the resources are also different.

■ **Read for Purpose**

1. **WHAT YOU KNOW**: What resources are found near your community?
2. **WHAT YOU WILL LEARN**: What is the geography of the Southwest like?

Much of the Southwest is very dry land where only cactus can grow.

THE DESERT

The climate of the Southwest is very dry. Much of the land is a desert (dez′ ərt), a very dry place where few plants will grow. Water is a precious resource in the desert. "We had strict rules for the use of water," said an Indian living in this area. "Even small children were taught to be careful."

Few animals are able to make their homes in the desert. This meant that the Anasazi could not depend on hunting to meet their need for food. Instead, they became farmers. Although the land of the Southwest is dry, the Anasazi learned to collect in ditches the little rain that fell. They used it to water their fields. That way they could grow corn, beans, and squash.

Farmers in the desert of the Southwest still use ditches to collect water for their fields.

A **mesa** is a landform shaped like a high, flat table. How many mesas can you find in this picture?

MESAS

The Anasazi built their houses in a special place in the desert. Throughout the Southwest there are many mesas (mā′ səs). A mesa is a landform made of rock and shaped like a high, flat table. In fact, *mesa* is the Spanish word for "table".

The Anasazi built their homes into the sides of a mesa. They grew their food on the top of the mesa. The fields made the mesa top look green. The name of the Anasazi community you will read about in the next lesson is Mesa Verde. *Verde* is the Spanish word for "green".

 Check Your Reading

1. What is a desert?
2. Why were the Anasazi farmers?
3. **GEOGRAPHY SKILL**: How did the geography of the Southwest affect the Anasazi?
4. **THINKING SKILL**: What are three questions you could ask to find out how the Anasazi grew food in the desert?

3 Mesa Verde, an Indian Community

READ TO LEARN

■ Key Vocabulary

kiva

■ Read Aloud

What was the village of Mesa Verde like? How did the Anasazi build their homes? What did the Anasazi children of Mesa Verde do for fun? Imagine yourself stepping into a time machine. Quickly you go back 100, 200, 300 years. Then the machine moves so quickly you cannot count the years. Finally, the machine stops. You step out into the village of Mesa Verde as it was almost 1,000 years ago.

■ Read for Purpose

1. **WHAT YOU KNOW**: Where would you go if you could travel in a time machine?
2. **WHAT YOU WILL LEARN**: What was life like in the community of Mesa Verde?

BUILDINGS AT MESA VERDE

The first thing you notice in Mesa Verde is a building that reminds you of an apartment house because it is so tall. The building is built into the side of the mesa. It has over 200 rooms, and more than 400 people live there.

The Anasazi build their homes from blocks of stones. In between the stones they put mud to hold the stones together. Now you notice something unusual about some of the buildings at Mesa Verde. They have square windows, but no doors. The Anasazi enter their houses by climbing up a ladder and through a hole in the roof. Then they bring the ladders inside to keep out unwanted visitors.

Each family in Mesa Verde has at least two rooms of its own. If a family is large, it may have more rooms. Some special rooms are shared by all the people in the community.

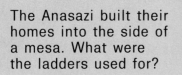

The Anasazi built their homes into the side of a mesa. What were the ladders used for?

RELIGION OF THE ANASAZI

Then you notice one of the shared rooms. Called a kiva (kē′ və), it is a special room used by the Anasazi for religious ceremonies. The kiva is a round room built below ground like a basement. It is used mostly by men. During your visit, some men are in the kiva praying for rain.

A kiva was a special room used for religious ceremonies.

DAILY LIFE

As you wander through Mesa Verde, you see that the people are very busy. Some of the women are making pots out of clay. Others are making baskets. Some men are sharpening stones to use as knives. Other men are watering fields on the mesa top.

Even the Anasazi children are busy. Some are grinding corn, while others are looking after the younger children. When they have time, they play tag.

The Anasazi children liked to play tag.

BACK TO THE PRESENT

Of course you cannot really travel back in time in a machine. But you can still visit Mesa Verde. The Anasazi no longer live there, but their culture was not lost.

Today the Zuñi (zü′ nyē) and Hopi (hō′ pē) Indians have kept some of the ways of the Anasazi. Find the Zuñi and Hopi Indians on the map on page 61. These Indians still live and work near the places where the Anasazi once lived.

Check Your Reading

1. Explain how the Anasazi built their houses.
2. What is a kiva?
3. **THINKING SKILL**: List the things that the Anasazi men do, the women do, and the children do.

70

4 A Visit to Mesa Verde Today

READ TO LEARN

■ Key Vocabulary

national park
museum
history

You can still visit the buildings the Anasazi built long ago at Mesa Verde.

■ Read Aloud

The Anasazi lived in Mesa Verde for a very long time. Then, they suddenly left. To this day no one is sure why. For many years Mesa Verde was forgotten.

Then, in 1888, two cowhands chasing some lost cows followed their tracks to the top of a mesa. All of a sudden they stopped in surprise. Ahead of them was an opening in the mesa, and in the opening was a building. They called the building they saw that day Cliff Palace. From then on the community of Mesa Verde was no longer forgotten.

■ Read for Purpose

1. **WHAT YOU KNOW**: Why do you think it took a long time for Mesa Verde to be found?
2. **WHAT YOU WILL LEARN**: What can be learned by visiting Mesa Verde today?

71

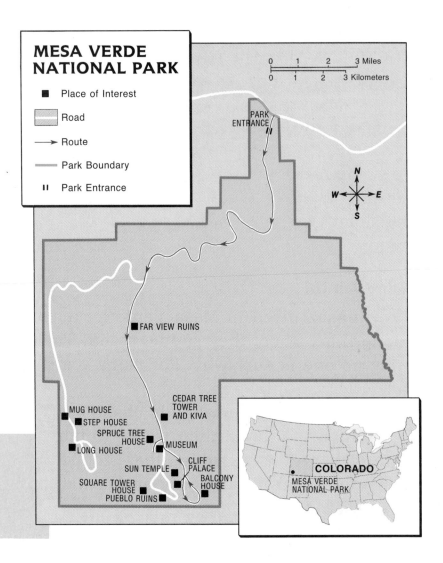

MESA VERDE NATIONAL PARK

- ■ Place of Interest
- ▨ Road
- → Route
- ▬ Park Boundary
- ‖ Park Entrance

0 1 2 3 Miles
0 1 2 3 Kilometers

PARK ENTRANCE

N W E S

■ FAR VIEW RUINS

CEDAR TREE TOWER AND KIVA

■ MUG HOUSE
■ STEP HOUSE
SPRUCE TREE HOUSE
■ LONG HOUSE
■ MUSEUM

SUN TEMPLE

CLIFF PALACE

SQUARE TOWER HOUSE
PUEBLO RUINS

BALCONY HOUSE

COLORADO
MESA VERDE NATIONAL PARK

MAP SKILL: In what state is Mesa Verde National Park located?

A NATIONAL PARK

Soon after this discovery, Mesa Verde was made a national park. A national park is land that is set aside for all the people in a country to enjoy. Mesa Verde National Park is shown on the map above.

Is there a national park near your community? Many beautiful parts of our country have been made into national parks. This way everyone can enjoy their special beauty.

The park rangers at Mesa Verde National Park show visitors around the park.

A TOUR OF MESA VERDE

A park ranger took Amelia Hubbell and her family around Mesa Verde. Use the map on page 72 to find the places they visited.

The first stop on the tour was the park's museum (mū zē′ əm). A museum is a building where people can go to look at interesting things. Amelia described what she saw in the museum.

We saw scenes showing how the Anasazi lived. One scene showed them building their houses into the mesa's side. We saw tools and baskets that they made. We also saw the clothes and jewelry they wore.

Amelia and her family enjoyed looking at jewelry made by the Anasazi in the museum at Mesa Verde.

After visiting the museum, the park ranger took the Hubbells to see Cliff Palace. Then they went to Balcony House. "This was my favorite part of the tour," said Amelia. "There were 40 rooms to explore. Then we climbed some stone steps and wooden ladders to the top of the mesa."

LEARNING ABOUT OUR HISTORY

Amelia learned many things by visiting the museum and buildings at Mesa Verde National Park. She learned about part of our country's history (his′ tər ē). History is the story of the past. Visiting places like Mesa Verde National Park is a good way to learn about our country's history.

Check Your Reading

1. Why have parts of our country been made into national parks?
2. Name three things Amelia saw at Mesa Verde National Park.
3. THINKING SKILL: Pretend you are taking a tour of Mesa Verde. What questions will you ask the park ranger?

74

KEEPING
CUSTOMS
ALIVE

Today the Pueblo Indians, like the Hopi and Zuñi Indians, live near the places the Anasazi once lived. Kathleen Correa is a Pueblo Indian. She lives at Isleta (ī lā′ tə) Pueblo in New Mexico. Kathleen is making sure the ways of the Pueblo Indians are not forgotten.

The teachers of the history and customs of the Pueblo Indians have always been the elders, or grandparents. The elders used to live with their adult children and help to care for their grandchildren. The young learned about Pueblo customs from their elders. Today, many houses are too small for the elders to live with their families. The customs of the Pueblo were no longer being passed on to children.

Kathleen has found a way to solve this problem. She brings together students and the Pueblo elders. The elders tell stories about their childhood. They explain how they were taught the Indian ways to be strong and healthy. They teach the children the Pueblo language and the dances used for feast days.

The most important part of the program is the storytelling. Joe Abeita (a bāt′ ə) is called Tata Fihtima (ta ta′ fīt a′ ma), or Grandfather, by the Indians at Isleta Pueblo. He tells stories about the past that he learned from his elders many years ago. These stories have always been used to teach. They are full of advice on how to be a good person.

Kathleen hopes that the children will learn what it means to be a Pueblo Indian. Then the beliefs and customs that have guided the Indians for hundreds of years will live on.

Comparing and Contrasting

Key Vocabulary

compare   contrast

To **compare** things is to see how they are alike. To **contrast** things is to see how they are different. Comparing and contrasting helps you learn more about things you see and hear.

For example, here are the telephone numbers of Amelia Hubbell's best friends. Amy's number is 735-2654. Nina's number is 735-4562.

They are alike because they have the same numbers. They are different because the numbers are not in the same order.

Trying the Skill

Compare and contrast the two pictures.

1. In what ways are the two pictures alike?
2. In what ways are they different?
3. What did you do to find your answers?

HELPING YOURSELF

One Way to Compare and Contrast	Example
1. Look at the first item.	Look at the tepee.
2. Choose something about it (size, shape, or use, for example).	The tepee is an Indian home.
3. Look at the other items to see if this is the same for all of them.	The second item is also an Indian home.
4. Repeat steps 1, 2, and 3.	The tepee is small. The building is big.
5. Tell how the items are alike and different.	The tepee and the building are both Indian homes. They are different in size.

Applying the Skill

Apply what you have learned by comparing and contrasting the pictures.

Read the following questions. Choose the best answer.

1. To compare and contrast the pictures you should first
   a. look at the first boy's clothes.
   b. guess the ages of the boys.
   c. find out where the boys live.
2. Both Indian boys are
   a. wearing shoes.
   b. wearing animal skins.
   c. carrying arrows.

Reviewing the Skill

1. What are some words that mean the same as *comparing?* The same as *contrasting?*
2. When might you use the comparing and contrasting skill at home?

IDEAS TO REMEMBER

- Every group of people has a culture—a way of life that includes their language, clothes, food, and religion.
- The Southwest has a desert climate where few plants and animals can live.
- The Anasazi built their homes into the side of a mesa in their community of Mesa Verde.
- Visiting places like Mesa Verde National Park is a good way to learn about our country's history.

REVIEWING VOCABULARY

culture   mesa
desert   museum
history

Number a sheet of paper from 1 to 5. For each word on the list above, write a sentence using the word correctly. The sentence should show that you know what the word means.

REVIEWING FACTS

1. Why are American Indians also called Native Americans?

2. Name an important natural resource of the Plains Indians. How was this natural resource an important part of their culture?

3. How did Mesa Verde get its name?

4. Copy the list below on a sheet of paper. Write **Anasazi** after those items that have to do with the Anasazi Indians, and **Plains** after the items that have to do with the Plains Indians.
   a. farming   e. tepees
   b. buffalo   f. Great Plains
   c. desert   g. mesa
   d. hunting   h. kiva

5. Why is visiting Mesa Verde a good way to learn about our country's history?

◖✎▶ WRITING ABOUT MAIN IDEAS

1. **Writing a Speech:** Write a brief speech explaining to second graders how the culture of the Anasazi Indians was affected by the natural resources of the Southwest.

2. Writing a Paragraph: Write two paragraphs. In the first paragraph tell two ways in which the Anasazi culture is like yours. In the second, tell two ways in which it is different from yours.

BUILDING SKILLS: COMPARING AND CONTRASTING

Use the pictures below to answer these questions.

1. What do you do when you compare and contrast?
2. Name two ways the pictures are the same.
3. What are two ways the pictures are different?
4. Why is it important to know how to compare and contrast?

STUDYING YOUR COMMUNITY

In Chapter 3 you read about Indians, the first Americans. Together with several of your classmates, find out about the Indians who used to live in your area. Learn what you can about their culture—the clothes they wore, the food they ate, and the houses in which they lived.

Then imagine that you could make a museum display about the lives of these early Americans. Decide what you would include in the exhibit. Make a drawing showing how you would arrange the displays. Write at least two sentences to explain each display to people visiting the museum.

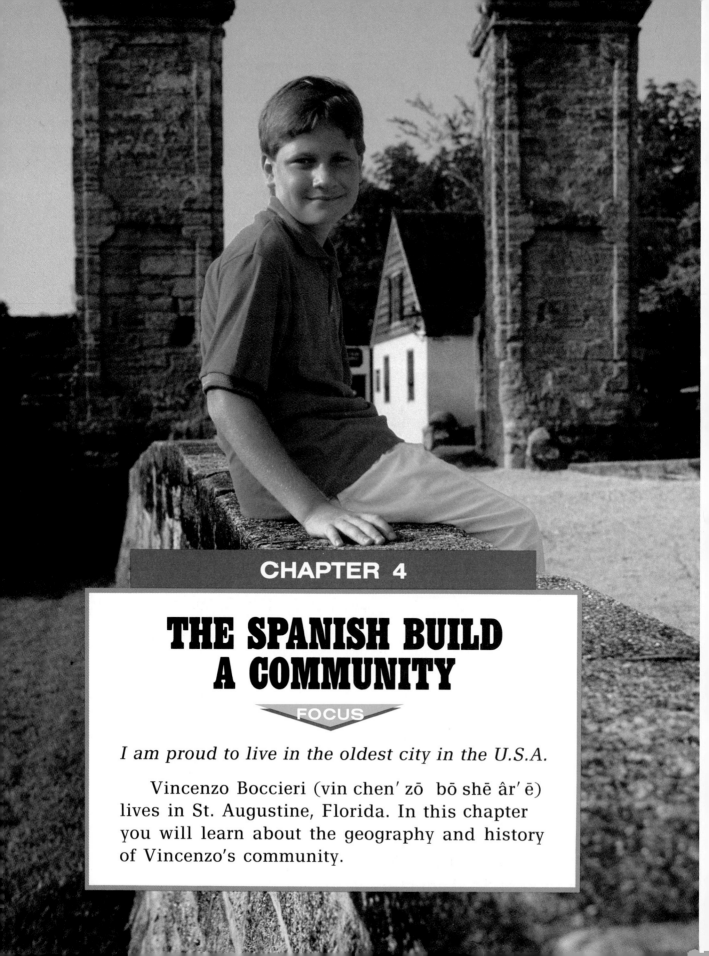

CHAPTER 4

THE SPANISH BUILD A COMMUNITY

FOCUS

I am proud to live in the oldest city in the U.S.A.

Vincenzo Boccieri (vin chen′ zō   bō shē âr′ ē) lives in St. Augustine, Florida. In this chapter you will learn about the geography and history of Vincenzo's community.

1 The Geography of St. Augustine

READ TO LEARN

◼ Key Vocabulary

island   harbor

peninsula   coquina

◼ Key Places

St. Augustine

◼ Read Aloud

St. Augustine is a community in the state of Florida. It is the oldest community in the United States built by people from Europe. These people came from Spain.

Why did the people from Spain choose to build the community of St. Augustine? You can start to answer this question by learning about the geography of St. Augustine.

St. Augustine is the oldest community in the United States built by Europeans.

◼ Read for Purpose

1. **WHAT YOU KNOW**: In what state is your community located?
2. **WHAT YOU WILL LEARN**: What is the geography of St. Augustine like?

FLORIDA

St. Augustine

ATLANTIC OCEAN

Gulf of Mexico

FLORIDA

0   100   200 Miles
0   100   200   300 Kilometers

St. Augustine

FLORIDA

MAP SKILL: The Spanish sailed to St. Augustine on ships like the one shown below. On what body of water is St. Augustine located?

THE LAND OF FLORIDA

For a long time both the Indians living in Florida and the people from Spain thought Florida was an island (ī′ lənd). An island is land with water all around it.

Most of Florida is really a peninsula (pə nin′ sə lə). A peninsula is land nearly surrounded by water. Look at the map above. What are the names of the bodies of water that nearly surround Florida?

A GOOD HARBOR

Look at the map of Florida again. Find the many places where the ocean goes into the land a little way. These places make good harbors (har′ bərz). A harbor is a protected place where ships are safe from

82

the ocean's waves. The Spanish built St. Augustine in a place with a good harbor so ships could easily load and unload goods.

NATURAL RESOURCES

Florida's good harbors are an important natural resource. Florida has many other natural resources. Have you ever heard Florida called the "Sunshine State"? What does this nickname tell you about the climate of Florida? Its warm and sunny climate is another important natural resource. It is the reason many older people move to Florida after they retire. Florida's climate is also good for growing citrus fruits like oranges and grapefruits.

Broken shells of small sea animals stick together to form coquina.

There is a special resource in the area around St. Augustine. It is called coquina (kō kē′ nə). Coquina is made up of the shells of very, very small sea animals. These shells stick together and form a very strong building material. In the next lesson you will see how coquina helped St. Augustine.

 Check Your Reading

1. How is a peninsula different from an island?
2. Name two of Florida's natural resources.
3. **GEOGRAPHY SKILL**: Look at the map on page 82. In what part of the country is Florida located?
4. **THINKING SKILL**: How is the geography of Florida different from the geography of the Southwest?

2 St. Augustine Begins

READ TO LEARN

Key Vocabulary

colony
colonist
trade

Key People

Pedro Menéndez
de Avilés

Key Places

Castillo de San
Marcos

Read Aloud

Gold, gold, and more gold. That is what the Spanish were hoping to find in Florida. They hoped that finding gold would make them rich and famous.

Most of the people from Spain did not find gold, and they did not get rich. But in 1565, one important person did find the place that is now St. Augustine. Building St. Augustine helped to make him famous.

Read for Purpose

1. **WHAT YOU KNOW**: Why do you think people first chose to come to your community?
2. **WHAT YOU WILL LEARN**: Why did the Spanish king want a colony in Florida?

The Granger Collection

This is one of the first maps of the St. Augustine area.

PEDRO MENÉNDEZ DE AVILÉS

It was Pedro Menéndez de Avilés (pā′ drō mə nen′ dəs dā ov′ ə lās) who found the place that became St. Augustine. Menéndez lived a life filled with adventure. When he was 14 years old he ran away from home to become a sailor. He fought against pirates. He made six trips to America.

No wonder the king of Spain wanted this brave man for a special job. The king wanted Menéndez to find a place to start a colony (kol′ ə nē). A colony is a place ruled by people from another country. A person who lives in a colony is called a colonist.

(*above*) Pedro Menéndez de Avilés started a colony at St. Augustine. (*below*) Colonists worked together to build a community.

Laying out of St. Augustine.

The Granger Collection

85

STARTING A COLONY

Why did the Spanish king want a colony in Florida? The king wanted the colony to protect Spanish trade. Trade is the buying and selling of goods. Spanish treasure ships carried gold, silver, and food from its colonies to Spain. They also brought goods from Spain to the colonies. Use the map below to follow the route these ships took.

Sometimes the ships were attacked near Florida by pirates from other countries. The king hoped a colony in Florida would protect Spanish trade by stopping the attacks.

MAP SKILL: Through what three bodies of water did Spanish trade ships travel to reach St. Augustine?

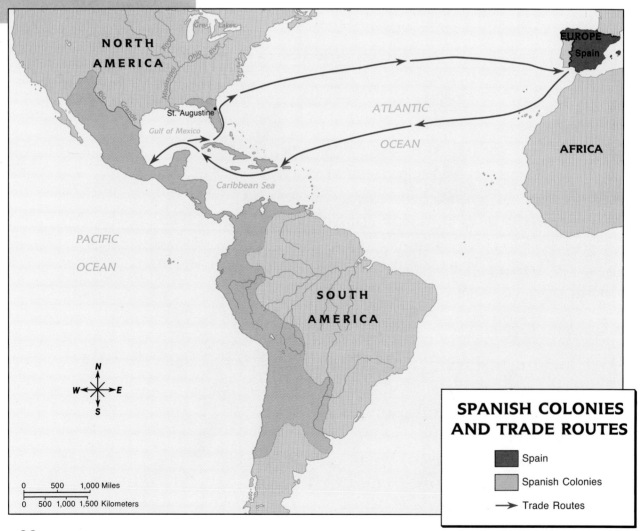

SPANISH COLONIES AND TRADE ROUTES

Spain

Spanish Colonies

→ Trade Routes

BUILDING ST. AUGUSTINE

The Spanish king told Menéndez to look for a good place for a colony. Menéndez chose St. Augustine. One reason Menéndez chose St. Augustine was its good harbor. As St. Augustine grew, coquina became important. The Spanish used coquina to build strong buildings.

One important building the Spanish built from coquina was Castillo de San Marcos (ka stē′ yō dā san mär′ kōs). This was the colony's fort. Soldiers could stand on the roof of the fort and look out to sea for pirate ships. Colonists could hide inside its walls when the colony was attacked.

You will read about St. Augustine today in the next lesson.

The Castillo de San Marcos is a fort that the Spanish built with coquina. Cannons helped protect the fort.

Check Your Reading

1. How did the Spanish use coquina?
2. **GEOGRAPHY SKILL**: Why did Menéndez think St. Augustine was a good place for a colony?
3. **THINKING SKILL**: How was Castillo de San Marcos like the buildings the Anasazi built at Mesa Verde?

Reading Time Lines

Key Vocabulary

time line

In the last lesson, you read about many important events that took place in St. Augustine. One way to find out when things happened is to use a time line. A time line can tell you the order in which events happened.

Reading Sarah's Time Line

Look at the time line below. It shows you three events in Sarah's life. You read time lines from left to right. The earliest event is on the left. The latest event is on the right. What event happened first on Sarah's time line? What event happened last?

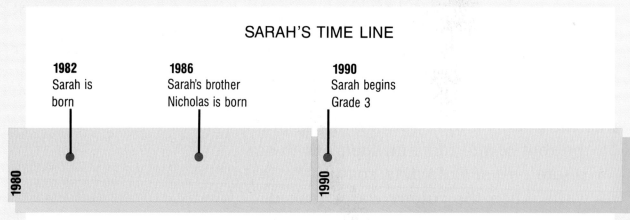

SARAH'S TIME LINE

1982
Sarah is born

1986
Sarah's brother Nicholas is born

1990
Sarah begins Grade 3

1980

1990

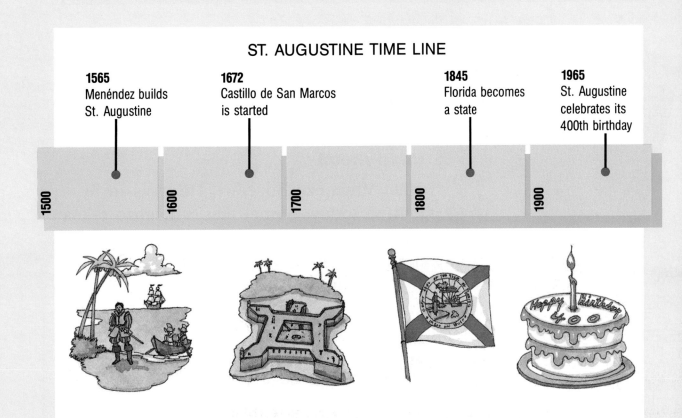

ST. AUGUSTINE TIME LINE

1565
Menéndez builds
St. Augustine

1672
Castillo de San Marcos
is started

1845
Florida becomes
a state

1965
St. Augustine
celebrates its
400th birthday

1500
1600
1700
1800
1900

Reading a Time Line in History

When you read about St. Augustine, you saw words such as "oldest," "for a long time," and "when he was 14 years old." All those words say something about time and when things happened.

The time line on this page shows 500 years, beginning with the year 1500. It shows four events in the history of St. Augustine, Florida.

Read the time line. Remember that the earliest events are on the left. What event happened first on the St. Augustine time line? When did it happen?

Reviewing the Skill

Use the St. Augustine time line to answer the following questions.

1. What is a time line?
2. When was Castillo de San Marcos built?
3. Was Castillo de San Marcos built before or after Florida became a state?
4. How do time lines help us to understand history?

3 A Visit to St. Augustine Today

READ TO LEARN

■ Key Vocabulary

tourist

■ Key Places

San Agustin Antiguo

■ Read Aloud

Meet Vincenzo Boccieri. He lives in St. Augustine today. Sometimes Vincenzo takes visitors to see the special places in his community. You can follow the tour they take on the map of St. Augustine below.

ST. AUGUSTINE

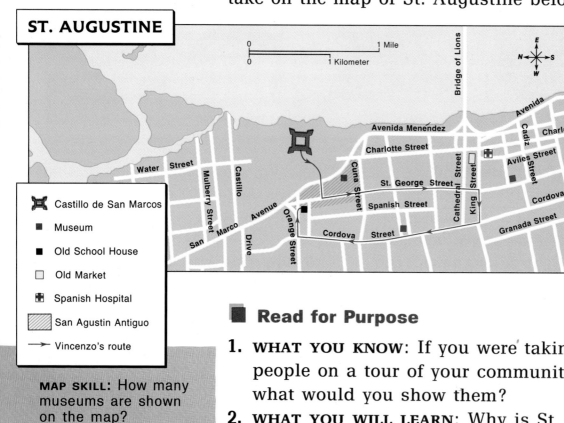

0 ——— 1 Mile
0 ——— 1 Kilometer

Bridge of Lions

Menéndez
Avenida
Avenida Menéndez
Charlotte Street
Cadiz
Charlotte Street
St. Francis Street
Aviles Street
Water Street
Castillo
Cuna Street
St. George Street
Cathedral Street
King Street
Cordova Street
Bridge Street
Mulberry Street
Spanish Street
San Marco Avenue
Orange Street
Cordova Street
Granada Street

Legend:
🏰 Castillo de San Marcos
■ Museum
■ Old School House
□ Old Market
✚ Spanish Hospital
▨ San Agustin Antiguo
→ Vincenzo's route

MAP SKILL: How many museums are shown on the map?

■ Read for Purpose

1. **WHAT YOU KNOW:** If you were taking people on a tour of your community, what would you show them?
2. **WHAT YOU WILL LEARN:** Why is St. Augustine called a "living history museum"?

TOURING ST. AUGUSTINE

The most famous place in St. Augustine today is the fort of Castillo de San Marcos. Its coquina walls are still guarding the harbor. Most of the tourists (tŭr′ ists) who come to St. Augustine visit the fort. A tourist is a person traveling on vacation. Vincenzo always starts his tour of St. Augustine at the fort.

As you can see on the map on page 90, Vincenzo next walks down St. George Street. St. George Street is in the Spanish Quarter. Reminders of the city's Spanish history are everywhere. Some streets, like Cordova and Granada, are named for cities in Spain. One street is named for the Spanish leader who founded St. Augustine. Can you find the name of this street on the map?

In the Spanish Quarter, Vincenzo and his friends talk with a woman dressed like a Spanish colonist.

THE LIVING HISTORY MUSEUM

Look at the map on page 90. Find
San Agustin Antiguo (san ô gus′ tin
an tē′ gwō). This is the oldest part of St.
Augustine. After visiting San Agustin
Antiguo, tourists understand why St.
Augustine is called a "living history
museum." Many of the houses here were
rebuilt to look like the original houses the
Spanish built.

Inside these houses you can see people
dressed in clothes like those worn by the
Spanish colonists. They are busy doing
things the same way colonists did. Some are
making candles or soap. Others are cooking
or weaving. Watching these people work
shows tourists what life was like in St.
Augustine long ago.

Vincenzo and his
friends watch a loom,
like the one above,
being made the way
the Spanish colonists
made them long ago.

PRIDE IN THE PAST

Each year more than one million tourists visit St. Augustine. Vincenzo and all the people in St. Augustine are proud of their community's history. They are happy to share it with the many tourists who visit St. Augustine each year.

The last place Vincenzo takes visitors is the Old School House.

Check Your Reading

1. What is a tourist?
2. How does St. Augustine help tourists learn about history?
3. **THINKING SKILL**: How is St. Augustine like Mesa Verde? How is it different?

CHAPTER 4 ▪ SUMMARY AND REVIEW

PEOPLE TO KNOW

Pedro Menéndez de Avilés
(1519–1574)

IDEAS TO REMEMBER

- A warm climate, a good harbor, and coquina are all important features of St. Augustine's geography.
- The Spanish built a colony at St. Augustine to protect Spanish trade.
- Tourists who visit St. Augustine can find out what life was like there long ago.

REVIEWING VOCABULARY

colony   peninsula
harbor   tourist
island

Number a sheet of paper from 1 to 5. Beside each number write the word from the list above that answers the question.

1. What is the name for land with water all around it?

2. What do you call a place ruled by people from another country?
3. What is the name for a person traveling on vacation?
4. What do you call land nearly surrounded by water?
5. What is the name for a protected place along the ocean where ships are safe from the waves?

REVIEWING FACTS

Number a sheet of paper from 1 to 5. Read each sentence. If the sentence is true, write **T** next to the number. If it is false, rewrite the sentence to make it true.

1. St. Augustine was started by Vincenzo Boccieri.
2. The king of Spain wanted a colony in Florida so colonists could search for gold.
3. St. Augustine was a good place for a colony because it had a good harbor.
4. The Castillo de San Marcos was made of coquina.
5. Today there is little left for tourists to see in St. Augustine.

✎ WRITING ABOUT MAIN IDEAS

1. **Writing a Paragraph:** Write a paragraph telling why St. Augustine's geography made it a good place for a Spanish colony.

2. **Writing an Advertisement:** Look at the photograph on page 81. Write a television advertisement telling tourists why they would enjoy visiting St. Augustine. The ad should make people want to visit this community.

BUILDING SKILLS: READING TIME LINES

1. How does a time line help you to order events?

2. How do you read time lines?

3. Look at the time line on page 89. When did Florida become a state? When did St. Augustine celebrate its 400th birthday?

STUDYING YOUR COMMUNITY

In Chapter 4 you read about St. Augustine and the tourists who visit this community. Every community has a place or places that would interest a visitor. It might be a home where a famous person once lived, or the spot where an important event took place.

Plan a tour of the interesting places in your community. Then write a booklet about the tour. The booklet should list the stops on the tour and tell something about them.

CHAPTER 5

THE PILGRIMS BUILD A COMMUNITY

FOCUS

I like living in Plymouth because of the people, the ocean, and the Mayflower II. The Mayflower II has given me the chance to understand how Plymouth started.

Nicole Mullen used these words to tell why she likes living in Plymouth, Massachusetts. In this chapter you will learn about Plymouth. You will read more about Nicole in Lesson 3.

1 The Geography of Plymouth

READ TO LEARN

■ Key Vocabulary

bay

■ Key Places

Plymouth
Plymouth Bay

■ Read Aloud

Do you know the answer to this riddle?

*If April showers bring May flowers,
What do May flowers bring?*

If you answered, "Pilgrims," then you guessed right.

The Pilgrims were colonists from England. They sailed from England on a ship called the *Mayflower*. In December 1620 they arrived at Plymouth in what is today the state of Massachusetts. Why did the Pilgrims choose Plymouth? This lesson will help you answer that question.

■ Read for Purpose

1. **WHAT YOU KNOW**: What body of water did the Pilgrims cross when they sailed from England to Plymouth?
2. **WHAT YOU WILL LEARN**: What is special about the geography of Plymouth?

The Granger Collection

The Pilgrims sailed from England to America on the *Mayflower* in 1620.

97

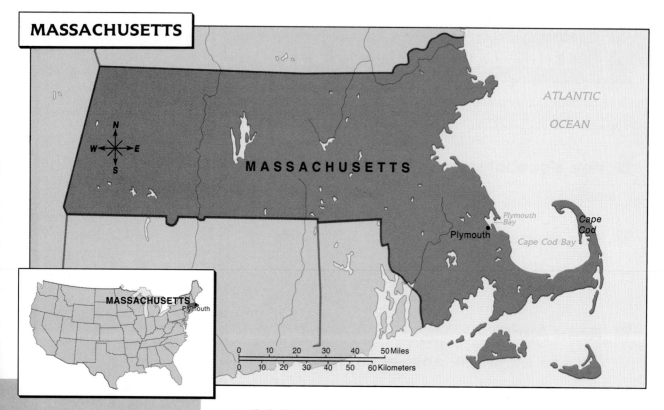

MASSACHUSETTS

MASSACHUSETTS

ATLANTIC

OCEAN

Plymouth Bay

Plymouth

Cape Cod Bay

Cape Cod

0 10 20 30 40 50 Miles
0 10 20 30 40 50 60 Kilometers

MASSACHUSETTS
Plymouth

MAP SKILL: In what part of our country is Plymouth located?

A GOOD HARBOR

Look at the map above. Notice the shape of the land near Plymouth. Do you see how land surrounds the water on three sides? A small body of water partly surrounded by land is called a bay. A bay is a good place for a harbor.

Plymouth is on a bay. Ships from Europe could bring supplies for the new community into Plymouth Bay. What other bay is shown on the map?

NATURAL RESOURCES

The Pilgrim leaders sent several men from the *Mayflower* to search for a place for their new home. The men found a flat area that had many streams of fresh water and was surrounded by forests. The land had already been cleared of trees by the Indians.

The water, the forests, and the cleared flat land were all important natural resources. The Pilgrims needed the water for drinking and cooking. They could grow food on the flat land. How do you think they could use the trees in the forests?

In the next lesson you will learn why the Pilgrims came to Plymouth, and how their community grew.

The Pilgrims chose the location for their community because of its many natural resources.

Check Your Reading

1. Who were the Pilgrims?
2. On what body of water is Plymouth located?
3. **GEOGRAPHY SKILL**: Name three natural resources found near Plymouth.
4. **THINKING SKILL**: How are the natural resources of Plymouth like the resources of St. Augustine? How are they different?

Using the Library

Key Vocabulary

fiction   dictionary
nonfiction   guide words
author   encyclopedia

Suppose your teacher asked you to find out more about the Pilgrims. Where would you go to look for the information? One answer is the library.

Finding Books in a Library

At the library you could find many books about the Pilgrims. Libraries divide books into fiction (fik' shən) and nonfiction. Fiction is about imaginary people, places, and events. A book of Paul Bunyan stories, for example, is fiction. Nonfiction is about real people, places, and events. A book that tells about the history of Plymouth is nonfiction.

Fiction and nonfiction books are placed in different parts of the library. Fiction books are grouped together in ABC, or alphabetical, order by the author's last name. An author is the person who wrote the book. To find the book of fiction called *Paul Bunyan,* by Steven Kellogg, you would look on the *K* shelves.

Books of nonfiction are grouped by subject, such as history or science. If you have trouble finding a book, ask the librarian for help. Librarians can help you find books even if you do not know the name of the book or the author.

Using a Dictionary

One useful library book is a dictionary (dik′ shən êr ē). A dictionary is a book that gives the meaning of words. It also tells you how to say the word. A dictionary lists words in alphabetical order.

Suppose you read this sentence in a book: "The Pilgrims were brave and hardy people." What does *hardy* mean? To look up *hardy* in the dictionary, first turn to the *H* words. Next use the two guide words on the top of each page to help you. The first guide word tells you the first word on the page. The second guide word tells you the last word on the page. All the words that come between the guide words will be on that page.

Using an Encyclopedia

Another useful library book is an encyclopedia (en sī klə pē′ dē ə). An encyclopedia is a book or set of books that gives information about people, places, things, and events. Many encyclopedias have drawings, maps, and photographs.

In an encyclopedia, as in a dictionary, subjects appear in

alphabetical order. Suppose you want to look up *Plymouth* in an encyclopedia. First you should find the book with a *P* on the cover. Encyclopedias also have guide words. You should use the guide words to find *Plymouth.*

Reviewing the Skill

1. Is a book about the geography of Plymouth fiction or nonfiction?
2. If you wanted to know the meaning of the word *bay*, where would you look?
3. Where would you look to find out more about the *Mayflower*?
4. How can knowing how to use the library help you to learn about history and geography?

2 Building Plymouth Community

READ TO LEARN

■ Key Vocabulary

harvest

■ Key People

Squanto
William Bradford

■ Read Aloud

When they arrived, the Pilgrims fell on their knees. They thanked God for bringing them over the great and dangerous ocean.

A Pilgrim leader wrote these words more than 300 years ago. His words tell us how important prayer was to the Pilgrims. In England they were not allowed to pray and worship God in their own way.

The Pilgrims wanted to live in a place where they could pray and worship God freely. So they decided to come to America to build a new community.

■ Read for Purpose

1. **WHAT YOU KNOW:** Make a list of three words that remind you of the Pilgrims.
2. **WHAT YOU WILL LEARN:** What people helped the Pilgrims to build their community?

This statue of a Pilgrim woman in Plymouth, Massachusetts, helps people remember the Pilgrims.

HELP FROM SQUANTO

You read in Lesson 1 that the Pilgrims chose Plymouth because of its natural resources. These natural resources helped the community to grow. But the Pilgrims needed other things to make their community grow. They needed help from the Indians who lived nearby.

An Indian named Squanto (skwän' tō) became a special friend. Before the Pilgrims came, Squanto had been kidnapped by sailors. He was taken to England where he learned English. After two years in England, he returned to his home. Squanto decided to live with the Pilgrims in Plymouth and to help them. Imagine how helpful he was. He taught the Pilgrims how to plant corn, and where to fish and hunt.

Squanto showed the Pilgrims where to hunt and fish. Squanto was a big help to the Pilgrims.

HELP FROM WILLIAM BRADFORD

To help Plymouth grow, the Pilgrims also depended on their leaders. William Bradford was one important and wise leader. He had many decisions to make.

One decision Bradford had to make helped to prevent a war. One time the Indians sent a strange message to Plymouth. The message was arrows in a snakeskin bag. Most of the Pilgrims wondered what the message meant. But Bradford knew the answer. He said the arrows meant the Indians were asking the Pilgrims if they wanted war.

The Pilgrims did not want war. They wanted peace. But Bradford knew they could not show fear. He filled the snakeskin bag with bullets and sent it back to the Indians. Bradford's message was, "We are not afraid. We will fight if we have to." Bradford made a good decision. The Indians understood his message and kept the peace.

William Bradford led the Pilgrims wisely. He helped to keep peace with the Indians.

The Granger Collection

HELPING EACH OTHER

The first winter at Plymouth was a sad and scary time for the Pilgrims. Many of them became sick, and almost half of them died. By the spring, things started to get better in the community. The Pilgrims worked together to plant corn and beans in the fields. They also built houses. The community began to grow.

By the fall, the Pilgrims' hard work made a difference. It was time to harvest (här′ vist), or pick, the crops they had grown. The Pilgrims had a big harvest. They knew they would have enough food to eat during the winter.

The Pilgrims worked together to build houses and to grow food.

The Granger Collection

A THANKSGIVING FEAST

William Bradford decided the community should celebrate their first harvest. The Pilgrims planned a huge feast. They invited the Indians who had been so helpful.

The feast lasted for three days. The Pilgrims cooked turkeys, ducks, and geese. There was plenty of corn and squash to eat. The Indians brought deer.

At the feast the Pilgrims gave thanks to God. They also thanked the Indians. The feast reminded the Pilgrims that they were a community. For them a community was a

The Pilgrims gave thanks to God at their Thanksgiving feast. They also gave thanks to the Indians for all their help.

Today families all over our country celebrate Thanksgiving each November.

place where people could depend on each other in good times and bad. When you celebrate Thanksgiving today, you are sharing a custom started by the Pilgrims.

 Check Your Reading

1. Why did the Pilgrims come to Plymouth?
2. Look at the list of words you made that remind you of the Pilgrims. Add three new words to the list.
3. THINKING SKILL: Make two lists. On one, list people who were important to the Pilgrims. On the other, list natural resources that were important.

107

3 A Visit to Plymouth Today

Today Plymouth, Massachusetts, is a busy, modern community. But visitors can still learn about its history. Fourteen-year-old Nicole Mullen will be your guide.

READ TO LEARN

Key Places

Plimoth Plantation

Read Aloud

Plymouth is very different today from the way it was when the Pilgrims arrived. Now it has many houses and buildings. Plymouth Bay is filled with many boats. But it is easy to learn about Plymouth's past. Visiting Nicole Mullen on the *Mayflower II* is one way to discover some of Plymouth's history.

Read for Purpose

1. **WHAT YOU KNOW**: Where can you go in your community to learn about its history?
2. **WHAT YOU WILL LEARN**: How can people learn about Plymouth's history?

ABOARD THE *MAYFLOWER II*

The *Mayflower II* is a ship in Plymouth Bay. It was built to look exactly like the first *Mayflower* on which the Pilgrims sailed to America.

Nicole works on the *Mayflower II*. Her job is to tell visitors about life aboard the *Mayflower*. Nicole tells the story of the Pilgrims' trip in a very special way. She acts the part of a girl who really did come to America on the *Mayflower*. The girl's name was Ellen More.

Nicole studied about the life of Ellen More. She dresses in clothes like those Ellen More wore. When tourists ask Nicole questions, she answers them just as Ellen might have long ago. Nicole even speaks in the way people spoke back then. When tourists ask her what her name is and how old she is, she says, "Me name be Ellen More. I myself be ten years of age."

Everything on the *Mayflower II* has been made to look the way it did on the first *Mayflower*.

Nicole also tells tourists how hard life was for the Pilgrims on the *Mayflower*. Day after day they ate hard bread and dried meat. Many people became sick. There was very little space, so almost everyone had to sleep on the floor. There was very little room for children to play. The Pilgrims' trip took two months.

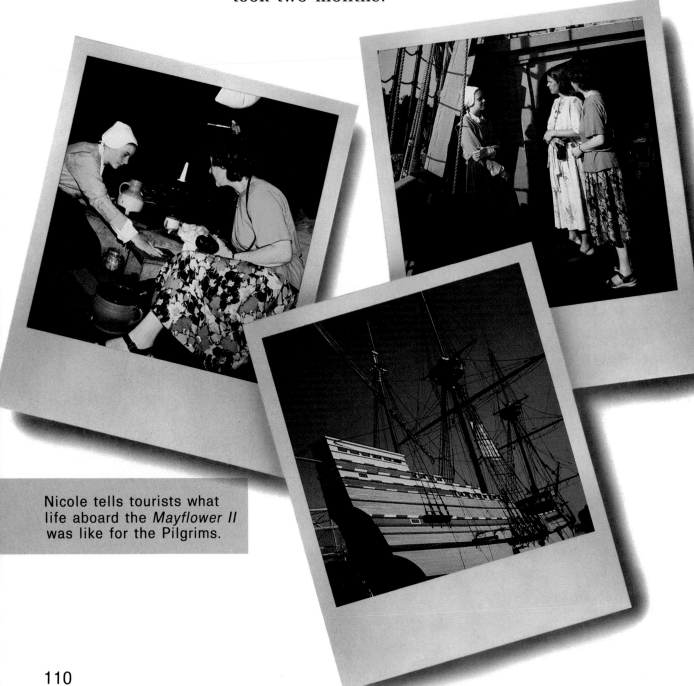

Nicole tells tourists what life aboard the *Mayflower II* was like for the Pilgrims.

PLIMOTH PLANTATION

The *Mayflower II* is just one part of the living history museum of Plymouth. The entire museum is called Plimoth Plantation. "Plimoth" is the way the first colonists spelled Plymouth.

Tourists who visit Plimoth Plantation say that visiting here is an easy way to learn history. It is like stepping back in time.

Everyone who works at Plimoth Plantation dresses and talks as the Pilgrims did.

Check Your Reading

1. Why is Nicole's job special?
2. What can be learned by visiting the *Mayflower II*?
3. **THINKING SKILL**: Describe what people can see at Plimoth Plantation.

PEOPLE TO KNOW

William Bradford (1590–1657)

Squanto (?–1622)

IDEAS TO REMEMBER

■ The Pilgrims chose to build a community at Plymouth because of its bay and other natural resources.

■ Indians helped the Pilgrims to survive in America by teaching them how to plant corn, and showing them where to fish and hunt.

■ People can visit the *Mayflower II* and Plimoth Plantation to learn about the history of the Plymouth community.

REVIEWING VOCABULARY

Number a sheet of paper from 1 to 5. Read the definition of each underlined word. Write **T** if the definition is true and **F** if it is false.

1. To <u>harvest</u> means to feast for three days.
2. A <u>bay</u> is land with water all around it.
3. A <u>bay</u> is land nearly surrounded by water.
4. To <u>harvest</u> means to pick crops that have grown.
5. A <u>bay</u> is a small body of water nearly surrounded by land.

REVIEWING FACTS

Number a sheet of paper from 1 to 5. Beside each number write the letter of the group of words that best completes each sentence.

a. a wise Pilgrim leader
b. colonists from England who settled in Plymouth
c. an American Indian who taught the Pilgrims how to get food
d. the ship on which the Pilgrims sailed from Europe to Plymouth
e. a tour guide at Plimoth Plantation

1. The Pilgrims were ———.
2. The *Mayflower* was ———.
3. Squanto was ———.
4. William Bradford was ———.
5. Nicole Mullen is ———.

✐ WRITING ABOUT MAIN IDEAS

1. **Writing a Paragraph:** Write a paragraph that uses two examples to show that William Bradford was a good leader.
2. **Writing a Letter:** Write a letter to Plimoth Plantation to find out more about what can be seen there in addition to the *Mayflower II.*
3. **Writing a Speech:** Pretend you work on the *Mayflower II.* Write a short speech in which you tell tourists what life was like aboard the *Mayflower.*
4. **Writing a Diary Entry:** Pretend you are a Pilgrim. It is the day after the Thanksgiving feast. Write an entry in your diary telling about the Thanksgiving celebration the Pilgrims shared with the Indians.

BUILDING SKILLS: USING THE LIBRARY

1. How are fiction books grouped in a library? How are nonfiction books grouped?
2. What steps would you use to look up the word *author* in a dictionary?
3. What is an encyclopedia? How are subjects listed in an encyclopedia?
4. Why is it important to know how to use the library?

STUDYING YOUR COMMUNITY

In Chapter 5 you read about the history of Plymouth. Find out about the early history of your community. Think of a way to make a "living history" museum that would teach visitors about your community's beginnings.

The museum might be a farm with the type of tools used by early farmers, a home that shows how people used to live, or an Indian village. Write two paragraphs describing your living history museum to visitors.

113

REVIEWING VOCABULARY

colony   peninsula
culture   tourist
history

Number a sheet of paper from 1 to 5. For each word on the list above, write a sentence using the word correctly. The sentence should show that you know what the word means.

((➔ WRITING ABOUT THE UNIT

1. **Writing a Speech:** Suppose you were planning a vacation. You could visit Mesa Verde, St. Augustine, or Plymouth. Which would you choose? Write a brief speech explaining your choice.

2. **Writing a Paragraph:** Make a list of words that describe the geography of the Southwest. Make a list describing the geography of Florida. Then write a paragraph explaining how the geography of the two areas is different.

3. **Writing a Letter:** Write a letter to an imaginary Anasazi child who is as old as you are. Tell him or her about ways that your lives are the same. Also tell about ways in which your lives are different.

ACTIVITIES

1. **Using the Library:** Choose one group of Indians shown on the map on page 61. Go to the library and find at least two books about the Indians you chose. Then write a paragraph explaining how you found the books and what you learned from them.

2. **Making a Time Line:** Make a time line of your life. You can use the time line on page 88 as a model. Start with the year you were born. Include two or three more events on your time line.

3. **Working Together to Get Information:** Write letters to the Chamber of Commerce of St. Augustine, Plymouth, and Mesa Verde to learn more about places of interest for tourists. Then use the brochures to make a bulletin board display for the class.

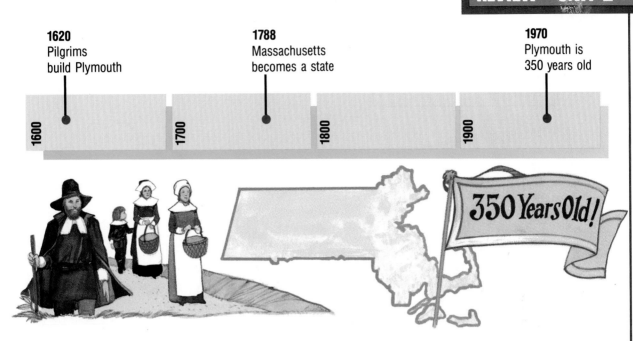

1620
Pilgrims
build Plymouth

1788
Massachusetts
becomes a state

1970
Plymouth is
350 years old

1600

1700

1800

1900

350 Years Old!

BUILDING SKILLS: READING TIME LINES

Use the time line above to answer the following questions.

1. How do you read a time line?
2. What happened first on the time line?
3. When did Massachusetts become a state?
4. When was Plymouth built?
5. What happened last on the time line?
6. How can time lines help you to understand history?

 **LINKING PAST, PRESENT, AND FUTURE**

In the future people might look for new places to live. They might build communities under the sea or in space. How could knowing about the history of Mesa Verde, St. Augustine, and Plymouth help people in these future communities? Describe at least two things they could learn.

3

TYPES OF COMMUNITIES

WHERE WE ARE

Communities are alike in many ways. They are all made up of people and have places where people live, work, play, and share special times. But there are also different types of communities. Some communities are large. Others are small. Communities depend on different natural resources. In this unit you will read about the different types of communities in which people live.

CHAPTER 6

COMMUNITIES HAVE DIFFERENCES

FOCUS

Tall modern buildings, noisy streets,
so much to see—
  The city's for me!

Quiet roads, forests, and farms—a country town
  Is where I can be found.
                              by Virginia Dooley

  These lines of poetry tell about a city and a town. How is a city different from a town? You will be able to answer this question after reading this chapter.

1 Living in Small Communities

READ TO LEARN

■ **Key Vocabulary**

rural area

■ **Key Places**

Valders, Wisconsin

■ **Read Aloud**

Do you know what kind of community you live in? There are several different kinds of communities. Size is one important way communities can be different.

In this lesson you are going to learn about small communities. You will meet Todd Borgwardt. Todd lives near the village of Valders, in the state of Wisconsin. As you read the lesson, try to decide if your community is like Todd's.

■ **Read for Purpose**

1. **WHAT YOU KNOW:** Is your community large or small?
2. **WHAT YOU WILL LEARN:** What is a rural area?

Todd lives in a village. A village is one kind of small community.

TOWNS AND VILLAGES

Todd lives on a farm near the village of Valders, Wisconsin. A village is usually the smallest kind of community. A town is another kind of small community. A town is bigger than a village. Like most towns and villages, Valders has a grocery store, a post office, and a school. The houses in Valders are far apart. About 1,000 people live in the village of Valders.

A RURAL AREA

Most towns and villages are located in rural areas. In a rural area communities are surrounded by forests or farms. Communities in rural areas are often far from each other.

Todd's family and the other people who live on farms surrounding Valders depend on the village for goods and services. Does Valders sound like the kind of community you live in?

In a rural area, towns and villages are often surrounded by farms.

DIFFERENT RURAL COMMUNITIES

The village of Valders where Todd lives is one kind of rural community. It is a farming community. The land around Valders is an important natural resource.

Rural communities are different because they have different natural resources. Not all communities in rural areas are farming communities. Some are logging towns. These communities are surrounded by forests. People in villages near the ocean often make their living by fishing.

Towns and villages are both small communities. They are also examples of rural communities. You will learn more about Todd and Valders in Chapter 7.

 Check Your Reading

1. Name two kinds of small communities.
2. Explain what a rural area is.
3. **THINKING SKILL:** To find out if someone lives in a rural area, which question would you ask? Why?
   a. Is your community surrounded by farms or forests?
   b. Is your community located near a river?

Sequencing

When you put things in order you are sequencing. To sequence you have to pay attention to what comes before a thing. You must also pay attention to what comes after it. For example, every year June comes before July. August comes after July.

Trying the Skill

Put the sentences about Todd in an order that tells a story. Then answer the questions.

A. Todd took the book home.

B. Todd's mother drove him to the library.

C. Todd chose a book from the fiction section.

1. Which sentence tells what happened first?

2. Which sentence tells what Todd did next?

3. How did you decide the order?

HELPING YOURSELF

One Good Way to Sequence	Example
1. Look at the information you have.	The sentences tell about Todd's trip to the library.
2. Choose the kind of order you want (by size, age, or time, for example).	You choose to put the sentences in order by time.
3. Choose one item from your information.	You might choose sentence **C**.
4. Choose the item closest to it to make the kind of order you want.	Sentence **B** tells what happened before sentence **C**.
5. Repeat step 4 until all the items are in the order you want.	Sentence **A** tells what happened after sentence **C**.

Applying the Skill

Sequence these sentences.

A. Todd puts a stamp on the envelope.

B. Todd mails his letter.

C. Todd writes a letter.

D. Todd puts his letter in an envelope.

Read the questions. Choose the best answer.

1. What kind of order did you use?
   a. time **b.** age **c.** size
2. What is the first sentence in the sequence you chose?
   a. A   **b.** B   **c.** any sentence
3. Which sentence tells what happened last?
   a. A **b.** B **c.** C
4. What is the correct sequence for these sentences?
   a. A, C, B, D
   b. C, D, A, B
   c. D, A, B, C

Reviewing the Skill

1. What do you do when you sequence?
2. What is one way you can follow to put things in sequence?
3. When have you used this skill before?

123

2 Living in Large Communities

READ TO LEARN

■ Key Vocabulary

suburb
urban area

■ Key Places

Seattle, Washington
Austell, Georgia
Atlanta, Georgia

SEATTLE, WASHINGTON

Amanda lives in a large community with many tall buildings. This building is called the Space Needle.

■ Read Aloud

Here is a post card Amanda Bronsky sent to one of her friends. It shows her community. Look at the post card. What is the name of the place where Amanda lives? Can you see ways that this community is different from the village of Valders?

■ Read for Purpose

1. **WHAT YOU KNOW:** Is your community as large as or smaller than the community Amanda lives in?

2. **WHAT YOU WILL LEARN:** What is an urban area?

124

A CITY

Amanda lives in the city of Seattle, Washington. About half a million people live in Seattle. There are many neighborhoods in Amanda's city. More people live in some of these neighborhoods than live in the whole village of Valders.

A city is like a small community in some ways. It has houses, stores, and schools just as a small town or village does. But it has many more of them. There are thousands of houses in Seattle. Most of these houses are close together. You read in Lesson 1 that Valders has a grocery store. Seattle has thousands of different kinds of stores.

Seattle can provide the people that live there with more goods and services than a town or village can. Does Amanda's community sound like your community?

Amanda likes going shopping with her mother. There are many stores in Seattle in which to shop.

Tiffany enjoys living in a suburb. There are many parks where she and her friends can play.

SUBURBS

Close to many cities you can find another kind of community called a suburb (sub' urb). A suburb is a community located near a big city. Tiffany Short lives in a suburb called Austell, Georgia. Austell is a suburb of the city of Atlanta, Georgia.

Austell is just one of many suburbs around Atlanta. Many people in these suburbs have jobs in Atlanta. Tiffany's mother works in Atlanta.

Tiffany calls her community an "in-between" community. Austell is bigger than a village or town, but not as big as a city. The houses in Austell are closer together than they are in a town, but not as close as they are in a city. Does the place where Tiffany lives make you think of your community?

URBAN AREAS

A city and the suburbs around it make up an urban area. More Americans live in urban areas than in rural areas.

Both Amanda and Tiffany live in urban areas. You will read more about Amanda and the city of Seattle in Chapter 8. In Chapter 9 you will read about Tiffany and life in the suburb of Austell.

Austell is part of an urban area. Austell is located near the city of Atlanta.

Check Your Reading

1. What is a suburb?
2. Explain what an urban area is.
3. **THINKING SKILL:** Is your community a city, a suburb, a town, or a village?

IDEAS TO REMEMBER

- A rural area is made up of small communities surrounded by forests or farms.
- An urban area is made up of a city and the suburbs around the city.

REVIEWING VOCABULARY

rural area   urban area
suburb

Number a sheet of paper from 1 to 5. Beside each number write the word or term from the list above that matches each definition. Some words can be used more than once.

1. A city and its suburbs
2. A community that is smaller than a city and larger than a village
3. An area in which towns and villages are located
4. A community that is located near a city
5. An area in which towns and villages are surrounded by farms or forests

REVIEWING FACTS

1. Name two kinds of small communities.
2. What are two facts about rural communities?
3. How do natural resources make rural communities different from each other?
4. In what ways is a city like a small community? In what ways is it different?
5. Why is the term "in-between" community a good description for a suburb?

WRITING ABOUT MAIN IDEAS

1. **Writing an Advertisement:** Write an advertisement that explains why people should visit your community. Your advertisement should tell whether your community is in an urban or a rural area.
2. **Writing a Paragraph:** In which kind of community would you rather live—rural, urban, or suburban? Write a paragraph explaining the reasons for your choice.

BUILDING SKILLS: SEQUENCING

Look at the pictures above. Then answer these questions.

1. What do you do when you sequence?
2. In what kind of sequence would you choose to put these pictures?
3. Write a correct sequence for the pictures. Give a reason for the sequence you chose.
4. How did you decide the sequence?

STUDYING YOUR COMMUNITY

On page 124 you saw a post card of Seattle, Washington. Design a post card of your community showing whether it is in an urban or a rural area. The post card might show the sight you think is most important. It might show an overall view of your community. Include the name of your community on the post card. Make a bulletin board display of the post cards your class makes.

129

CHAPTER 7

RURAL COMMUNITIES

FOCUS

What I like the most about living in Valders is the Valders Picnic. There are all kinds of contests. It gives me a chance to show off my farm skills.

Todd Borgwardt lives near the farming community of Valders, Wisconsin. In this chapter you will learn about Valders, and about other rural communities.

1 Farming Communities

READ TO LEARN

■ Key Vocabulary

dairy farm

■ Read Aloud

Do you know what black and white cows are called? If you lived in Valders, Wisconsin, you would. They are called Holsteins (hōl' stēnz). The people in Valders know this because they live in a farming community.

You read in Chapter 6 that a farming community is one kind of rural community. There are different kinds of farms and farming communities. There are large farms where many different machines are needed to do the work. Other farms are small family farms. Some are vegetable farms, while others are fruit farms. There are also farms where farmers raise animals. In this lesson you will learn why farms are different.

■ Read for Purpose

1. **WHAT YOU KNOW:** Name three different kinds of rural communities.
2. **WHAT YOU WILL LEARN:** How are farms different from one another?

There are many different kinds of farms. Some farmers grow crops. Others raise animals.

131

DIFFERENT RESOURCES

Why do farmers grow or raise different things? Natural resources, such as climate, water, and soil, are important reasons. Farms in different parts of our country have different natural resources. So farmers use these resources to grow different things.

For example, the good soil of the Great Plains is just right for growing wheat. So is the climate. It is hot in the summer and cold in the winter. If you visited the Great Plains you would see many wheat farms. But citrus fruits need a warm climate all year long. Places with a warm climate, such as California and Florida, have many citrus farms. Climate helps farmers decide what to grow.

Climate is important in deciding what to grow. Citrus fruits, like oranges, grow best in warm climates.

Many farmers raise animals, such as cows, sheep, or poultry. Poultry are birds such as chickens or turkeys that are raised for their meat or their eggs. Sheep are raised for their meat or their wool. Farms where cows are raised for their milk are called dairy farms. Many dairy farms are located in grassy areas because grass is an important natural resource for dairy farmers. They need the grass to feed their cows. You will learn more about dairy farming in the next lesson.

There are many sheep ranches in the western part of the United States. Some states have more sheep than people.

 Check Your Reading

1. What is a dairy farm?
2. **GEOGRAPHY SKILL:** Why are farms different in different parts of our country?
3. **THINKING SKILL:** Make a list of the foods you have eaten today. On what kinds of farms would these foods have been grown?

READ TO LEARN

■ Key Vocabulary
pasture

■ Key Places
Valders

■ Read Aloud

Todd Borgwardt's father wakes him up every day at five o'clock in the morning. Todd wishes he could sleep later, but he knows the cows on his parents' dairy farm are waiting for him. The cows need to be milked. Todd's dairy farm is a family farm. Everyone in the family cooperates to run the farm.

Every morning Todd helps his father milk the cows on their dairy farm.

■ Read for Purpose

1. **WHAT YOU KNOW:** What is a dairy farm?

2. **WHAT YOU WILL LEARN:** What is life like on a dairy farm?

FARMING IN WISCONSIN

The map on this page shows you dairy-farming areas in the United States. Notice the large dairy-farming area in Wisconsin. Wisconsin has more dairy farms than any other state in our country. This is because Wisconsin has many grassy areas that provide food for dairy cows.

Find the community of Valders on the map. Todd Borgwardt's dairy farm is located near the community of Valders.

MAP SKILL: The grassy land around Valders is perfect for dairy farming. Name a state in the northeastern part of the United States where there are dairy farms.

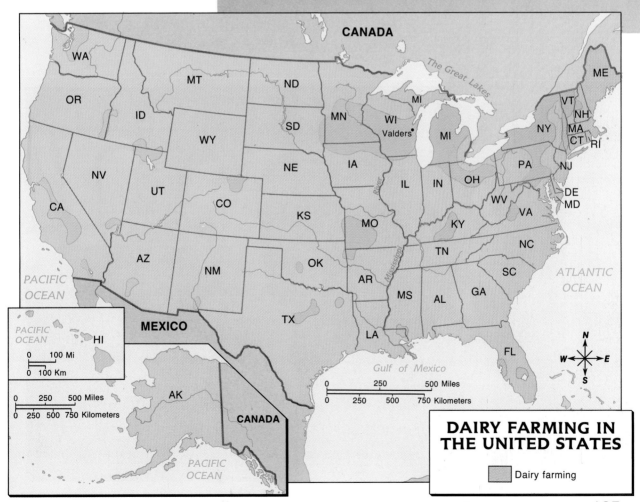

DAIRY FARMING IN THE UNITED STATES

Dairy farming

135

MILKING THE COWS

The Borgwardt farm has about 100 cows that need to be milked every day. Milking the cows is a big job. Luckily, Todd's family has special machines to help them. The milking machines take milk from the cows and pump it through a pipe into a big tank. The tank is very cold inside. This keeps the milk cool so it will not spoil or get sour.

After the cows are milked, Todd and his father clean the milking machines. These machines must be ready for the evening milking. After he finishes school, Todd helps his father milk the cows again. The cows are always milked twice a day—early in the morning and in the evening. Imagine how much work that is!

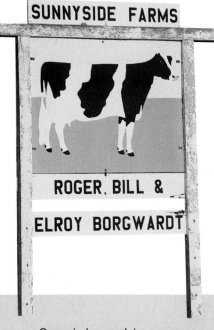

Special machines are used to milk the cows.

FOOD FOR THE COWS

Todd and his sister Jennifer also help
feed the cows. Cows are big eaters.
Most of the year the cows eat grass in
the fields on the farm. Fields of grass
that animals feed on are called
pastures (pas' chərz).

During the winter, it is too cold
and snowy for the cows to eat in the
pastures. Todd and Jennifer help bring
corn, oats, and hay to the cows in the
barn. Todd's family grows all of the
food it feeds the cows.

During the winter,
Todd and Jennifer
help to feed the cows.
The cows eat hay,
corn, and oats.

HAVING FUN

Farm families work hard, but they also have time for fun. Todd and his family like driving into Valders to go to the library or to eat in restaurants. But some of the things the Borgwardts enjoy doing are especially for people living in a farming community.

For example, one of Todd's favorite events is the Valders Picnic. Once a year people in the community get together for a day of races, games, and contests.

Todd says, "My favorite contest is the sack race." Everyone has fun at the picnic.

Some people come to the Valders Picnic to look at new farm tractors. Todd likes the hay-stacking contest and the sack-jumping contest the best.

✔ Check Your Reading

1. What is a pasture?
2. How are the cows on Todd's farm fed?
3. **GEOGRAPHY SKILL:** Look at the map on page 135. What state is south of Wisconsin?
4. **THINKING SKILL:** Make two lists. On one, list the jobs that Todd does on the farm. On the other, list the ways he has fun.

3 From Farm to You

READ TO LEARN

Key Vocabulary

producer
consumer

Read Aloud

"Okay, it's time to decide," said Lauren Everett's father.

"Mushrooms," said Lauren.

"No," her brother Ricky answered. "Plain cheese."

"Boring, boring. How about pepperoni?" Lauren asked.

Have you guessed what Lauren's family is doing? They are ordering a pizza. A special kind of cheese is used to make pizzas. It is called mozzarella (mot sə rel' ə). Mozzarella cheese is one of the things made from the milk from Todd's farm. Let's see how milk from Todd's farm is made into cheese.

Read for Purpose

1. **WHAT YOU KNOW:** Name two things made from milk.
2. **WHAT YOU WILL LEARN:** How is milk made into cheese?

FROM FARM TO DAIRY

In the last lesson you read that the milk on Todd's farm is stored in a special tank. Once a day, a truck arrives at the Borgwardt farm. The driver takes out a long hose and connects it to the tank. The milk is pumped into the truck's cold tank. Then the truck takes the milk to a dairy in a nearby town.

The dairy is a producer, or maker, of dairy products. Dairy products are made from milk. Cheese is just one dairy product. The chart on this page shows you other dairy products.

CHART SKILL: This chart shows you some of the many dairy products made from milk. Did you eat a dairy product today? What was it?

DAIRY PRODUCTS

Yogurt

Milk

SKIM MILK

WHOLE MILK

Butter

Cheese

COTTAGE CHEESE

Ice cream

ICE CREAM

AT THE DAIRY

Cheese making starts at the dairy. First, workers pour the milk into special machines. These machines heat the milk and then cool it quickly. This kills any germs in the milk that might make people sick. This process is called pasteurization (pas chə rə zā' shən).

Next, the milk is pumped into very large pans. In these pans, part of the milk becomes solid and part water. The water part, called the whey (wā), is removed from the pan. The solid part is called the curd. Curd is used to make cheese.

Giant spoons stir the curd. Workers then use machines to stretch and pull the curd into long, flat shapes.

Workers follow many steps when they make cheese from milk.

FROM DAIRY TO CONSUMERS

Finally, workers cut the cheese into smaller pieces. Then they wrap it in plastic. The cheese is then loaded onto delivery trucks.

Some of the cheese is taken to stores where consumers can buy it. Consumers are people who buy and use products. You are a consumer when you buy food to eat or clothes to wear. Some of the cheese is also bought by restaurants. Todd's farm is hundreds of miles from the pizza restaurant where Lauren's family is eating. But you could say that Todd's family and Lauren's family have a connection—the cheese on the pizza.

When people buy cheese in a store, they are consumers of dairy products.

 Check Your Reading

1. What is a consumer?
2. Add three dairy products to your list of things made from milk.
3. **THINKING SKILL:** List in correct order the steps used to make cheese.

142

A Rural Community in Canada

READ TO LEARN

■ Key Vocabulary

province
prairie

■ Key Places

Estevan
Saskatchewan
Canada

■ Read Aloud

Dear Todd,

Last week our teacher gave us a list of students in the United States who wanted pen pals. I picked your name. My name is Margaret McDonald, and I live on a wheat farm in the country of Canada. My teacher said to tell you about myself and my community.

■ Read for Purpose

1. **WHAT YOU KNOW:** In what country would you like to have a pen pal?

2. **WHAT YOU WILL LEARN:** How is Margaret's farm in Canada alike and different from Todd's farm in Wisconsin?

143

A FARM ON THE PRAIRIE

My family's wheat farm is near the town of Estevan, in the province of Saskatchewan (sas kach' ə won). A province is a part of Canada. It is like a state in the United States.

Estevan is a good place for wheat farming because it is on the prairie (prâr' e). A prairie is flat land that was once covered with grass. Prairie soil is good for growing wheat.

The climate in Estevan is also good for growing wheat. Wheat needs rain, but not too much rain. Too much rain can spoil our wheat.

Wheat is used to make flour. Bread, cereal, and rolls are products made from wheat flour. When you eat a bowl of cereal, it might be made from the wheat on our farm.

MAP SKILL: This map shows wheat farming areas in Canada. In what provinces would you see wheat farms?

WHEAT FARMING IN CANADA

Wheat farming

WORK AND FUN

Running a wheat farm is hard work. My two brothers and I help my parents after school and during the summer. But we also have a lot of fun together.

My brothers and I like to go to the movies in Estevan. Once a year my family goes to the rodeo. At a rodeo there are contests to see who can ride a bull longest. There are other riding and roping contests, too. The rodeo is lots of fun.

Well, that's enough about me for now. Please write to me soon about where you live.

Your friend,
Margaret

Rodeos are popular in Canada and the United States. What are other ways Americans and Canadians are alike?

✔ Check Your Reading

1. Name three products made from wheat.
2. Why are there many wheat farms near Estevan?
3. **GEOGRAPHY SKILL:** Describe the geography of Estevan.
4. **THINKING SKILL:** How is Margaret's farm like Todd's farm? How is it different?

Reading Flow Charts

Key Vocabulary

flow chart

Do you remember the first time you learned to play a new game? You had to learn all the rules of the game. You also had to learn what steps to follow, and the order in which to follow them.

An easy way to learn about something that has many steps is to use a flow chart. A flow chart shows all the steps in an activity.

It shows in what order the steps are done, too.

Getting Ready for School

Every morning when you get ready for school, you go through certain steps. You probably do these steps in the same order every day. The flow chart below shows eight steps Adam follows in order to get ready for school.

Notice the arrows on the flow chart. Follow the arrows to see

GETTING READY FOR SCHOOL

Wake up.

Wash up.

Get dressed.

Gather homework and books.

Brush teeth.

Eat breakfast.

Put on coat.

Walk out door.

MAKING CHEESE

Milk is taken to dairy.

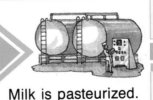

Milk is pasteurized.

Milk is poured into pans.

Cheese is stretched.

Spoons stir the solid part.

Milk becomes part solid and part water.

Cheese is wrapped.

Cheese is taken to stores.

which step comes first, second, third, and so on. What is the first step on the flow chart? What is the last step Adam follows?

A Flow Chart About Making Cheese

The flow chart on this page shows the steps that are used to make milk into cheese. What is the first step on the flow chart?

With your finger, trace the rest of the steps on the flow chart. Follow the arrows that show the order of the steps. How many steps are there altogether?

Reviewing the Skill

Use the Making Cheese flow chart to answer these questions.

1. What is a flow chart?
2. What happens after the milk is poured into pans?
3. Make a flow chart that shows something you do every day. It might show what you do each day after school. Remember to use arrows to show the order of the steps.
4. Why is a flow chart a good way to learn about something that has many steps?

IDEAS TO REMEMBER

- Farmers in different parts of the country grow or raise different things because their farms have different natural resources.
- Dairy farms need large grassy areas called pastures on which the cows can feed.
- Milk is used to make cheese and other dairy products.
- Wheat farms need a climate that is not too rainy and prairie soil that is good for growing wheat.

REVIEWING VOCABULARY

consumer   producer
pasture   province
prairie

Number a sheet of paper from 1 to 5. Beside each number write the word or term from the list above that best completes each sentence.

1. A _____ is flat land that once was covered with grass.
2. When people buy products they are _____.
3. A large grassy area on which animals such as cows feed is called a _____.
4. A dairy is a _____ of milk products.
5. A _____ is a part of Canada, like a state in the United States.

REVIEWING FACTS

1. Why is climate important to farmers?
2. What is a dairy farm?
3. Name two jobs a child on a dairy farm might do.
4. In what area of the country are most of America's dairy farms located? Why?
5. What are three jobs that workers might have in a dairy that makes cheese?
6. What happens when milk is pasteurized?
7. Name three examples of dairy products.
8. What natural resources help wheat to grow?
9. Why is Estevan a good place for growing wheat?
10. What do people do at a rodeo?

✏️ WRITING ABOUT MAIN IDEAS

1. **Writing a Menu:** Write a lunch menu filled entirely with foods that are dairy products and wheat products.
2. **Writing a How-to Paragraph:** Write a how-to paragraph about the making of milk into cheese.
3. **Writing a Letter:** Pretend you are Todd Borgwardt. Write a letter back to Margaret McDonald in Canada telling her what life is like on a dairy farm in Wisconsin.

BUILDING SKILLS: READING FLOW CHARTS

1. Explain how to read a flow chart.
2. In the flow chart on page 147, what happens after the milk is taken to the dairy?
3. What is the first step shown in the flow chart? What is the last step in the flow chart?
4. Why is a flow chart a good way to explain how cheese is made?

STUDYING YOUR COMMUNITY

In Chapter 7 you read about different kinds of farming communities. Do people in your community produce farm products or consume them, or do both?

Think of what you ate for breakfast. What farm products were part of those foods? From what parts of the country might the farm products have come? Have you ever visited a rural area? If so, what was it like? How was it like your community? How was it different? Write the answers to these questions in a paragraph.

CHAPTER 8

URBAN COMMUNITIES

▼ FOCUS ▼

Seattle is a beautiful city. Pike Place Market is my favorite part of the city, but I like to visit the museums and parks, too.

This is how Amanda Bronsky described Seattle. Seattle is one of the urban communities you will read about in this chapter. You will read more about Amanda in Lesson 2.

1 Urban Communities and Resources

READ TO LEARN

■ Key Vocabulary

port
industry

■ Key Places

Chicago, Illinois
Denver, Colorado

■ Read Aloud

Nathan Katzin was drawing red circles on a map of the United States.

"What are you doing to that map?" asked his sister Rachel.

"I'm doing my schoolwork," said Nathan. "My teacher asked us to find ten large cities in our country."

"That's not so hard. I think I could do that," answered Rachel.

"But that's not all," said Nathan. "We also have to tell why so many people came to live in these cities."

Nathan and his sister Rachel are finding large cities on a map of the United States.

■ Read for Purpose

1. **WHAT YOU KNOW:** What is the largest city close to your community?
2. **WHAT YOU WILL LEARN:** Why do cities grow?

151

CITIES AND RESOURCES

Rachel looked at the map. "Most of these cities are near lakes, rivers, or the ocean."

"Exactly!" said Nathan. "Water is an important natural resource. Many cities grew because they are near water. Chicago, Illinois, for example, is on Lake Michigan. Its location helped it become a busy port. You probably know that a port is a place where ships load and unload goods."

"I see," said Rachel. "But why did Denver, Colorado, grow? It isn't located near water. It isn't a port."

MAP SKILL: This map shows the 25 largest cities in the United States. Which large city is northeast of New York City?

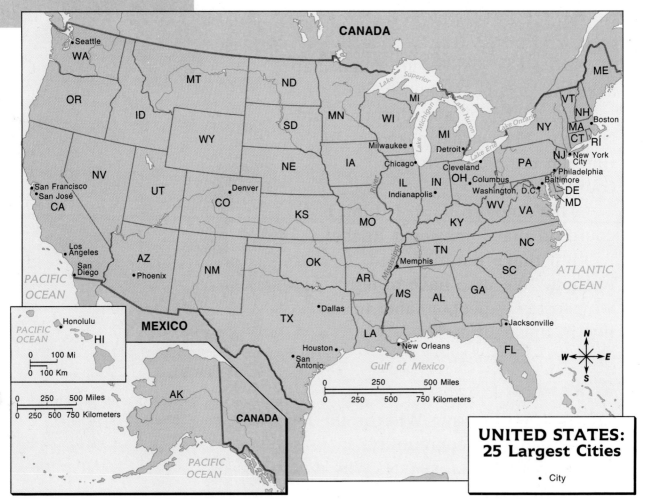

**UNITED STATES:
25 Largest Cities**

· City

"Other resources help cities grow, too," said Nathan. "Denver began as a mining community. People first went to Denver to find gold and silver. But many people stayed in Denver because they liked another one of Denver's resources—its beautiful mountains."

Today Denver is a beautiful, modern city. It began as a mining community after gold and silver were discovered in the nearby mountains.

CITIES AND PEOPLE

Nathan began to fold up his map.

"Wait," said Rachel. "You've forgotten to mention what I think is a city's most important resource!"

"What's that?" asked Nathan.

"People," said Rachel. "People are needed to build cities. They are needed to run  industries (in' dəs trēz). I learned that an industry is the many businesses that make one product. For example, businesses that make coats and pants are part of the clothing industry. Hotels and tour guides are part of the tourist industry."

"Cities do need people," said Nathan. "I think I'll put people first on my list."

✔ Check Your Reading

1. List three resources that help cities to grow.
2. What resource helped Chicago to grow? How did it help?
3. **GEOGRAPHY SKILL:** Look at the map on page 152. Name five large cities in the Northeast of our country.
4. **THINKING SKILL:** Name an industry located near your community.

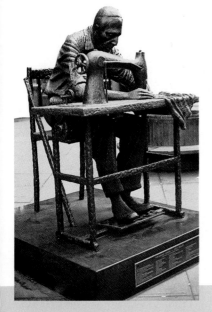

(*above*) This statue was made to honor the many people who work in the clothing industry in New York City. (*right*) A worker pushes clothing racks along a street in New York.

SAVING PIGEON CREEK

Several years ago, an excited student from Jackson Elementary School saw a salmon (sam'ən) swimming in Pigeon Creek. Pigeon Creek is a small stream located north of Seattle, near the community of Everett. That salmon was the first one anyone had seen in the creek in ten years. The return of the salmon meant that five years of hard work by the students at Jackson Elementary had made a difference.

For many years salmon had returned to Pigeon Creek each year to lay their eggs. But then things began to change around Pigeon Creek. Pigeon Creek became so dirty that salmon stopped returning to it.

Students from Jackson Elementary School decided to change this. They decided to "adopt" Pigeon Creek.

The first thing the students did was to ask their school to buy an aquarium, or glass tank. The aquarium was filled with water, and used to raise thousands of salmon eggs. When the eggs hatched, the students released them into Pigeon Creek.

After releasing the eggs, the students still had a big job to do. They had to make sure Pigeon Creek was kept clean. The students worked together to let the people in their community know about Pigeon Creek and the salmon. They put up signs near the creek that said "DON'T DUMP." The creek was cleaned up to get rid of any litter.

Almost every day a student from the school went to the creek to make sure it was kept clean. At last the students' hard work made a difference. The salmon returned to Pigeon Creek.

155

Reading Bar Graphs

Key Vocabulary

bar graph
population

Have you ever heard the saying that one picture is worth a thousand words? A good way to learn about the communities in which we live is to look at graphs. This is because a graph lets you see information in picture form.

In this lesson, you will study a kind of graph called a bar graph. A bar graph uses bars of different lengths to show amounts.

Reading the Graph

To use a bar graph, first read its title. What is the title of the graph on this page? The title tells you that this graph shows the population (pop yə lā' shən) of the rural and urban areas of the United States. Population is the number of people who live in a place.

Look at the bottom of the graph. It shows two types of areas in which people live. Look at the numbers on the left side of the graph. The numbers stand for the numbers of people living in these areas.

Now "read" the graph. First find the bar for Rural Areas. Move your finger to the top of the bar. Then slide your finger across to the number at the left. Your finger should be just below the number 60 million. The population of the rural areas of the United States is a little less than 60 million.

Now find the bar for Urban Areas. About how many people live in the urban areas of the United States?

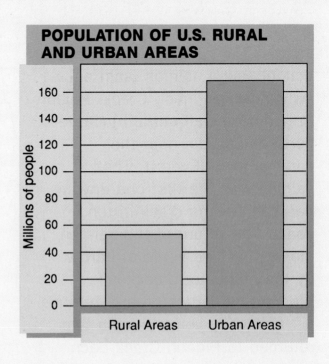

POPULATION OF U.S. RURAL AND URBAN AREAS

156

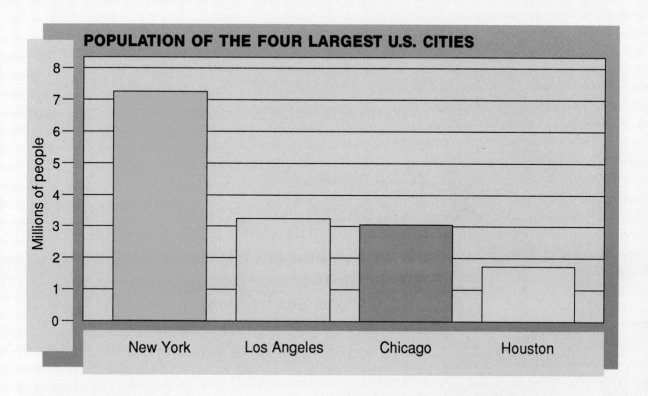

POPULATION OF THE FOUR LARGEST U.S. CITIES

Millions of people

New York   Los Angeles   Chicago   Houston

A Bar Graph of United States Cities

Now look at the bar graph on this page. What is its title? This bar graph shows the population of the four largest cities in the United States. Four bars are used to show this information.

Look at the bottom of the graph. What does it show? Look at the numbers on the left side of the graph. What do they stand for? Which city has the largest population? What is the population of this city?

Reviewing the Skill

Use the bar graph on this page to answer the following questions.

1. How do you read a bar graph?
2. Which city has the smallest population? What is the population of this city?
3. Do more Americans live in Houston or Chicago? Do fewer Americans live in Los Angeles or Chicago?
4. How can a bar graph help you to learn?

2 Seattle, an Urban Community

READ TO LEARN

■ Key Vocabulary

central business district

■ Key Places

Puget Sound
Seattle

■ Read Aloud

In the last lesson you learned some of the reasons why cities grow. But what is it like to live in a city? What do people in a city do for fun?

Let's find out by visiting someone who lives in a city. Amanda Bronsky is eight years old. She lives in an apartment with her mother in the city of Seattle, Washington.

"Seattle is the largest city in the state of Washington," says Amanda. "It is also the largest city in the northwestern part of our country."

■ Read for Purpose

1. **WHAT YOU KNOW:** What are two things that help cities to grow?
2. **WHAT YOU WILL LEARN:** What is the city of Seattle like?

This is Amanda's house in Seattle. What kind of house does she live in?

158

Seattle is located on Puget Sound. Salmon fishing is an important industry in the city.

SEATTLE'S RESOURCES

Seattle is an important port because of its location on Puget (pū' jit) Sound. Puget Sound is part of the Pacific Ocean.

Seattle's location near the ocean has made fishing a big industry there. Many people work at jobs catching salmon and other fish.

Seattle's mild, wet climate is another resource. "I like living where it never gets very hot or very cold," Amanda says. "The rain keeps the trees and grass green all the time."

CENTRAL BUSINESS DISTRICT

Amanda's family lives near Seattle's central business district. This is the busy part of the city where most of the office buildings, stores, hotels, and restaurants are located. People work at many different jobs in the central business district.

HAVING FUN IN SEATTLE

There are special places in Seattle to have fun. You can find some of these places on the map below. Amanda's favorite places are the Pacific Science Center and Pike Place Market. Amanda likes to climb into a spacecraft at the Science Center and pretend she is a space traveler. At Pike Place Market, she likes to look at the arts and crafts people are selling. Her mother buys fresh fruits, fish, and flowers at the market.

Amanda's family likes to do some of the same things in Seattle that Todd's family does in the rural community of Valders.

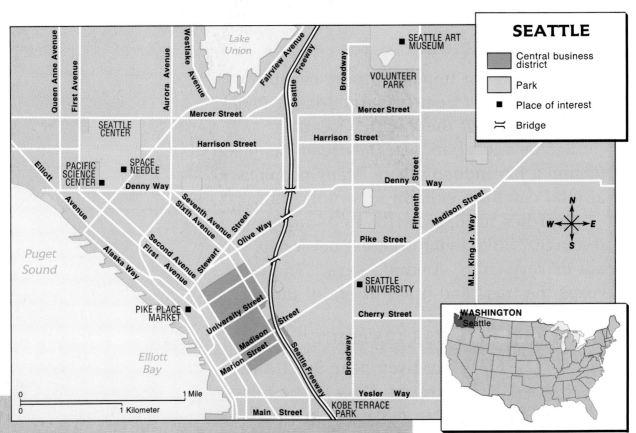

MAP SKILL: Find the Pacific Science Center on the map of Seattle. Is it located in the central business district?

Amanda likes to shop with her mother at Pike Place Market. At the Pacific Science Center, she pretends she is a space traveler.

Both families like to go to the movies and to eat in restaurants. But because Amanda lives in a city, she has a choice of more movies and restaurants. Since they are close to her home, she and her mother can walk or take a bus to reach them.

Check Your Reading

1. What are two resources that helped Seattle to grow?
2. What is the central business district?
3. **GEOGRAPHY SKILL:** How has Seattle's geography made a difference in this city?
4. **THINKING SKILL:** How is Seattle different from Todd's community of Valders?

3 Manufacturing in Seattle

READ TO LEARN

■ Key Vocabulary

factory   assembly line

These airplanes were made in Seattle in the building behind them. It is the largest building in the world.

■ Read Aloud

Amanda's mother works in a special building near Seattle. It is the biggest building in the world. It is so big that 58 football fields could fit inside it! The building has to be this big because airplanes are made there. Making airplanes is an important industry in Seattle.

■ Read for Purpose

1. **WHAT YOU KNOW:** Name another industry that is important in Seattle.
2. **WHAT YOU WILL LEARN:** How does an assembly line work?

162

A FACTORY

Amanda's mother works in a factory (fak′ tər ē). A factory is a building where goods are manufactured, or made.

At the airplane factory, most workers have one special job to do. Every worker does the same job on each airplane that he or she works on. For example, some workers put the seats in the planes. Others attach the wheels. These workers are on an assembly line. An assembly line is a line of workers who put together parts of a product.

Workers on the assembly line each have one job to do when they build an airplane.

MAKING AN AIRPLANE

Trains bring computers, seats, and other parts for new airplanes to the factory in Seattle. The parts come from as far away as New York and Canada. The trains come right into the factory on special tracks.

When all the parts for one airplane are in the factory, workers like Amanda's mother are ready to begin building an airplane. The flow chart shows you some steps in making an airplane.

MAKING AN AIRPLANE

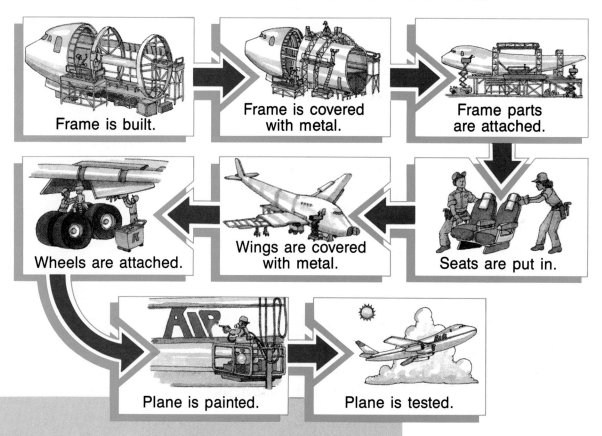

Frame is built.

Frame is covered with metal.

Frame parts are attached.

Wheels are attached.

Wings are covered with metal.

Seats are put in.

Plane is painted.

Plane is tested.

CHART SKILL: This chart shows how an airplane is put together. What is the last step?

 Check Your Reading

1. What is a factory?
2. What is an assembly line?
3. **THINKING SKILL:** What three questions could you ask to learn more about making airplanes?

An Urban Community in Mexico

READ TO LEARN

■ Key Vocabulary

capital

■ Key Places

Mexico City
Mexico

Amanda writes in her journal every day.

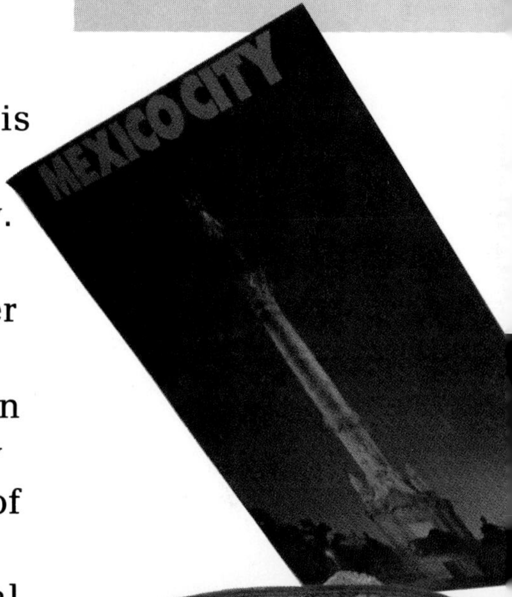

■ Read Aloud

Amanda Bronsky has a journal, which is a kind of diary. Every night before she goes to bed, Amanda writes about her day. She pretends she is writing to a friend. Keeping a journal helps Amanda remember her thoughts and her feelings.

Amanda visited Mexico City on vacation last summer. Mexico City is in the country of Mexico. Mexico is located to the south of the United States. You can read about Amanda's trip to Mexico City in her journal.

■ Read for Purpose

1. **WHAT YOU KNOW:** If you could visit a city on vacation, where would you go?
2. **WHAT YOU WILL LEARN:** What is life like in Mexico City?

Friday

I am *so excited*. Tomorrow our family is going to Mexico City on vacation. We will visit our friends, the Perez family. Their daughter Carmen is my age. My Mom says that Mexico City is the capital of Mexico. A capital is a place where leaders of a country or state meet and work. I know that the capital of the United States is Washington, D.C. It will be fun to visit Mexico's capital.

Saturday

Our friends met us at the airport and took us first to see Mexico City's central business district. Like the central business district in Seattle, there are many office buildings, shops, hotels, and restaurants.

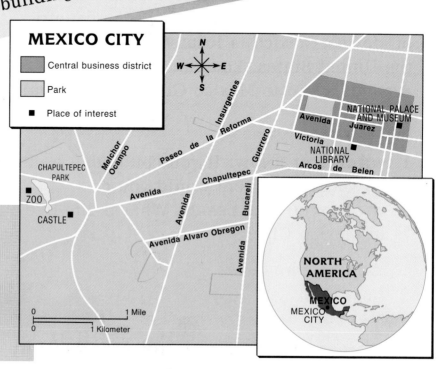

MEXICO CITY

- Central business district
- Park
- ■ Place of interest

N W E S

NATIONAL PALACE AND MUSEUM

Avenida Juarez

Victoria

NATIONAL LIBRARY

Arcos de Belen

Insurgentes

Paseo de la Reforma

Melchor Ocampo

Guerrero

Bucareli

Chapultepec

CHAPULTEPEC PARK

Avenida

Avenida

Avenida

Avenida Alvaro Obregon

ZOO

CASTLE

0   1 Mile
0   1 Kilometer

NORTH AMERICA

MEXICO

MEXICO CITY

MAP SKILL: The National Palace and Museum is a popular place in Mexico City. In what direction is this museum from Chapultepec Park?

166

Sunday

This has been the BEST day of our vacation. We visited Carmen's favorite place in the city—Chapultepec (chə pül' tə pek) Park. There is so much to do there! The park has a zoo and an old castle. We saw a panda at the zoo. The castle is now a museum where we learned about the history of Mexico.

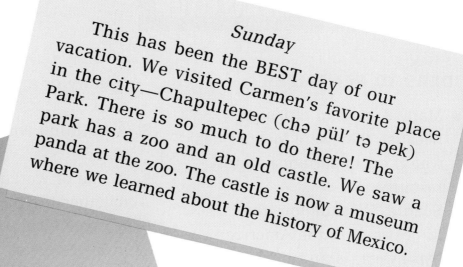

Chapultepec Castle is now a museum visited by many tourists.

Monday

This is the last day of our vacation. Carmen taught me how to say good-by in Spanish—adios (ä dē ōs'). Everyone in Mexico speaks Spanish. I felt sad saying adios, but I am glad I had a chance to visit Mexico City.

 Check Your Reading

1. Explain what a capital is.
2. List three places to visit in Mexico City.
3. **THINKING SKILL:** How is Mexico City like your community? How is it different?

167

IDEAS TO REMEMBER

■ Many American cities grew because they were located near water, an important natural resource.

■ Seattle, Washington, the largest city in the American Northwest, is an important port with a big fishing industry and a mild, wet climate.

■ Each factory worker on an assembly line has one special job in the putting together of parts to make one big product.

■ Mexico City, the capital of Mexico, is like Seattle in many ways.

REVIEWING VOCABULARY

assembly line	industry
capital	port
factory	

Number a sheet of paper from 1 to 5. Beside each number write the word or term from the list above that best matches each definition.

1. The many businesses that make one product
2. A place where the leaders of a country or a state meet and work
3. A building where goods are made
4. A line of workers who put together the parts of a product
5. A place where ships load and unload goods

REVIEWING FACTS

Number a sheet of paper from 1 to 5. Read each sentence below. If the sentence is true, write **T** next to the number. If it is false, rewrite the sentence to make it true.

1. The one reason that cities grow is because they are located near rivers, lakes, or oceans.
2. Seattle's natural resources include the Pacific Ocean and a hot, dry climate.
3. An important industry in Seattle is the making of airplanes.
4. Pike Place Market is an exciting place to visit in Seattle.
5. Chapultepec is the capital of Mexico.

WRITING ABOUT MAIN IDEAS

1. **Writing a Legend:** Write your own legend, or story, about how Seattle was started. Mention the city's natural resources in your story.

2. **Writing a Paragraph:** Write a paragraph about the ways in which Seattle and Mexico City are the same and the ways in which they are different.

3. **Writing a How-to Paragraph:** Write a how-to paragraph telling about the steps in making an airplane.

BUILDING SKILLS: USING BAR GRAPHS

Use the bar graph on this page to answer the questions below.

1. What is the correct way to read the graph to find out how many people live in urban areas?

2. About how many people live in rural areas?

3. Do more people live in rural areas or in urban areas?

4. Why is a bar graph a good way to show information?

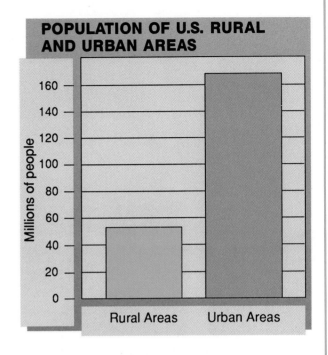

POPULATION OF U.S. RURAL AND URBAN AREAS

Millions of people

Rural Areas   Urban Areas

STUDYING YOUR COMMUNITY

In Chapter 8 you read about cities and industries. Find out about industries in or near your community. Does the industry make products or provide services? If it makes products, what are they? What kinds of jobs do people do?

Choose one of the industries. How many people work in it? How did it help your community to grow? If possible, plan a trip to a factory or other place related to the industry.

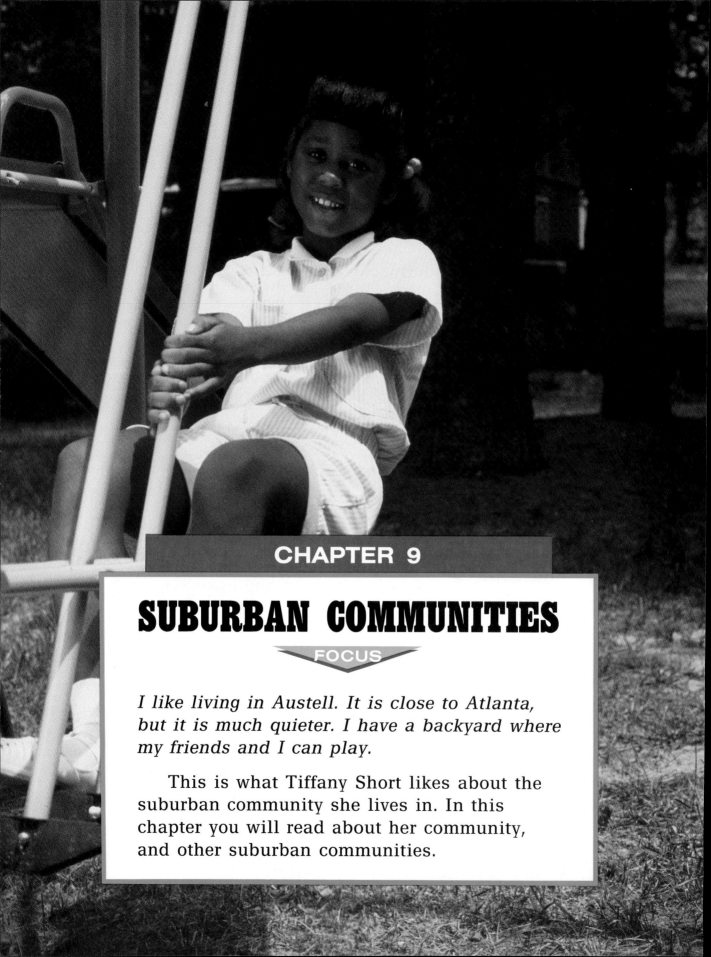

CHAPTER 9

SUBURBAN COMMUNITIES

FOCUS

I like living in Austell. It is close to Atlanta, but it is much quieter. I have a backyard where my friends and I can play.

This is what Tiffany Short likes about the suburban community she lives in. In this chapter you will read about her community, and other suburban communities.

1 Suburban Communities

READ TO LEARN

■ Key Vocabulary

transportation

■ Key Places

River Forest, Illinois

■ Read Aloud

"Good morning, folks," said the radio announcer. "It's time for the rush hour traffic report. Cars and buses are moving very slowly on all roads into the city this morning. Traffic is backed up all the way to the bridge."

Does this kind of traffic report sound familiar to you? It might if you live in a city or one of its suburbs.

■ Read for Purpose

1. **WHAT YOU KNOW:** What is a suburb?
2. **WHAT YOU WILL LEARN:** How are suburbs alike?

Many people in suburbs use highways to travel into nearby cities. Helicopter pilots report traffic problems on the highways.

171

SUBURBS ARE ALIKE

Traffic reports like this sound very familiar to Luke Martino. Luke and his family live in River Forest, Illinois. River Forest is a suburb of Chicago. Like thousands of other people living in the suburbs around Chicago, Luke's parents work in Chicago. They travel back and forth from their home in River Forest to Chicago every workday.

People who live in suburbs often travel to work in a nearby city. This is one way suburbs are alike. Suburbs are also alike because they all have stores where people shop and homes where people live. Suburbs are usually less crowded than cities.

Suburbs are less crowded than cities. Many people in suburbs travel to a nearby city to work.

TRANSPORTATION

One very important way suburbs are
alike is that they all depend on good
transportation (trans pər tā′ shən).
Transportation is the moving of people and
products from place to place. Cars, buses,
trains, trucks, and planes are all kinds of
transportation. Suburbs need good
transportation to connect them to nearby
cities.

In the next two lessons you will read
about Austell, Georgia. Austell is a suburb
of Atlanta. Atlanta is the largest city in
Georgia. It is also the capital of Georgia.
You will find out about transportation
between Austell and Atlanta. You will also
find out what life is like in a suburb.

People who live in
the suburbs need
transportation to get
them to their places of
work in the city.

Check Your Reading

1. Explain what transportation is.
2. What are two ways suburbs are alike?
3. **THINKING SKILL:** What kinds of
   transportation are found in your
   community?

2 A Suburb in Georgia

Tiffany and her family live in the suburb of Austell. Does the main street in Austell remind you of your community?

READ TO LEARN

■ Key Vocabulary

commuter

■ Key Places

Austell

■ Read Aloud

Several years ago the place where Tiffany Short now lives was a farm field. Farmers grew cotton on the land where Tiffany's house now stands. Back then Austell was a small town. Then the city of Atlanta began to grow, and so did Austell. Austell became a suburb of Atlanta. Today Austell is part of the Atlanta urban area.

In Lesson 1 you learned that suburbs are alike. How is Austell like River Forest, Illinois? People in both suburbs travel to larger cities to work. Many people in Austell now work in Atlanta. Let's find out what life is like in the suburb of Austell by visiting Tiffany Short.

■ Read for Purpose

1. **WHAT YOU KNOW:** What is an urban area?
2. **WHAT YOU WILL LEARN:** What is life like in the suburb of Austell, Georgia?

174

EASY TO LIVE IN

As Atlanta grew, it became busier and more crowded. People started moving from Atlanta to Austell and other smaller communities near the city. Tiffany's family moved to Austell.

"Quiet, friendly, and easy to live in." This is how Tiffany describes her community. "I can walk to my school, and I have a backyard where my friends and I can play."

Tiffany's parents like living in Austell. There are many shopping malls where they can buy clothes and other goods. Tiffany has more room to play. "We still like to visit Atlanta," says Tiffany's mother. "But we also like staying in Austell to work in our garden and to visit friends."

Tiffany and her family like to shop in the mall in Austell. There are many stores and fun events in the mall.

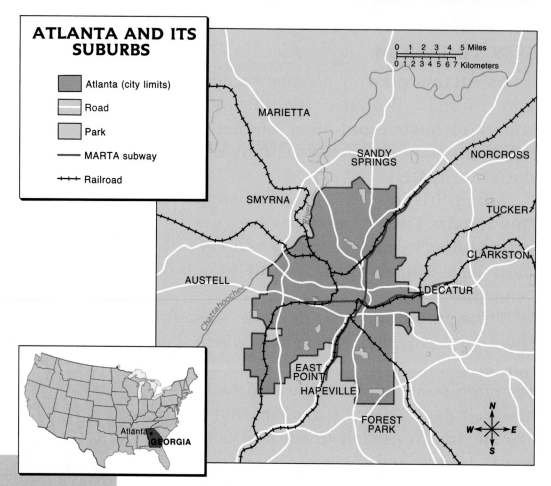

ATLANTA AND ITS SUBURBS

Legend:
- Atlanta (city limits)
- Road
- Park
- MARTA subway
- +++ Railroad

0 1 2 3 4 5 Miles
0 1 2 3 4 5 6 7 Kilometers

MARIETTA

SANDY SPRINGS

NORCROSS

SMYRNA

TUCKER

CLARKSTON

AUSTELL

DECATUR

Chattahoochee River

EAST POINT

HAPEVILLE

FOREST PARK

N E S W

Atlanta

GEORGIA

MAP SKILL: This is a map of Atlanta and the suburbs nearby. In what direction is Austell from Atlanta?

A COMMUTER

Tiffany's father owns a cleaning business. He works in Austell and other suburbs close to it.

Tiffany's mother is a commuter (kə mūt′ ər). This means she travels back and forth every workday from Austell to her job in Atlanta. In the next lesson you'll find out how Tiffany's mother commutes between Austell and Atlanta.

Check Your Reading

1. Why does Tiffany feel Austell is easy to live in?
2. What is a commuter?
3. **THINKING SKILL:** List three questions you could ask to find out more about Austell.

176

3 Transportation and Suburbs

READ TO LEARN

■ Key Vocabulary

subway
public transportation

■ Read Aloud

Getting to work used to be the worst part of the day for Tiffany's mother. She had to drive to work on a crowded highway. Commuting often took more than 30 minutes because of all the traffic. The Atlanta urban area had grown very quickly. The roads connecting Atlanta with its suburbs had become very crowded. Transportation into and out of Atlanta was one of the city's biggest problems.

Every workday Tiffany's mother commutes from Austell to Atlanta.

■ Read for Purpose

1. **WHAT YOU KNOW:** How do most people in your community travel from place to place?
2. **WHAT YOU WILL LEARN:** How does public transportation help cities and suburbs?

177

PUBLIC TRANSPORTATION

How did Atlanta solve its transportation problem? MARTA is one answer. MARTA is the name for the Metropolitan Atlanta Rapid Transit Authority. It is made up of buses and subways, or underground trains.

MARTA is a public transportation system. All the people in the community can use public transportation. Other kinds of transportation, such as cars or bicycles, are private transportation.

Thousands of commuters use MARTA's public transportation system of buses and subways to go to and from work.

178

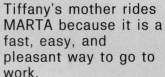

Tiffany's mother rides MARTA because it is a fast, easy, and pleasant way to go to work.

"Riding MARTA is faster and cheaper than taking my car," says Tiffany's mother. Commuting only takes her ten minutes now. As more people ride MARTA, fewer cars are on the highways. MARTA has helped Atlanta grow by providing an easier and more pleasant way for people to travel.

MARTA has also helped Austell and the other suburbs of Atlanta to grow. Roads, trains, and buses are all important ways of connecting suburbs with cities. Suburbs cannot grow without good transportation.

Check Your Reading

1. What is public transportation?
2. How did MARTA help Atlanta to solve its transportation problem?
3. **THINKING SKILL:** Sort all the different kinds of transportation you know of into two groups—private and public.

Reading Transportation Maps

Key Vocabulary

transportation map

You read in this chapter that MARTA helped Atlanta solve its transportation problems. How could you find out MARTA's routes? You could use a transportation map. A transportation map is a special map that shows how you can travel from one place to another.

There are many different kinds of transportation maps. Some show you roads. Road maps are used by people traveling by car. They show the many different roads that go between places. People can use them to find the best way to travel between two cities, for example.

Other transportation maps show railroad lines, air routes, ship routes, or subway and bus routes. In this lesson you will learn about a transportation map that shows subway and bus routes in Atlanta.

If you wanted to use public transportation to get around Atlanta, you could use the MARTA map shown on the next page. You know that MARTA is both bus and subway transportation. Many people, like Tiffany Short's mother, travel by bus to a MARTA subway station. Then they ride the subway to a stop close to where they work.

Using a MARTA Map

In order to understand and use the MARTA map, you must first study the map key. The map key shows you the symbols for MARTA subway lines and stations. Subway lines are shown in red. There are two subway lines—a North–South line and an East–West line. There are many stations along both of these lines. What symbol shows a subway station?

This map also shows some of the important roads in the Atlanta area. The blue lines show the routes of buses which take people to MARTA subway stations. Each bus route is labeled with a number. These numbers are

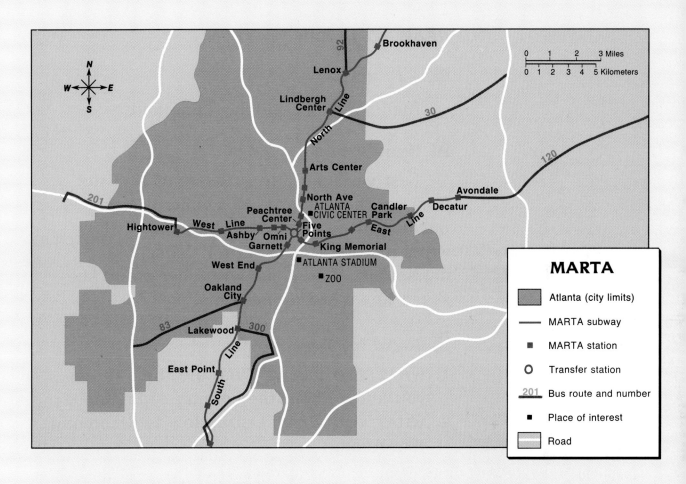

Map legend:

MARTA

- Atlanta (city limits)
- MARTA subway
- MARTA station
- Transfer station
- 201 Bus route and number
- Place of interest
- Road

shown in blue. When Tiffany's mother commutes into Atlanta to work, she takes a bus to the Hightower subway station, on the West Line. What is the number of the bus she takes?

Reviewing the Skill

Use the MARTA map to answer the following questions.

1. What are transportation maps?
2. What is the number of the bus that travels to the Oakland City station on the South Line? What is the number of the bus that travels to the Lindbergh Center station on the North Line?
3. At what MARTA subway station does the North-South line cross the East-West line? What MARTA subway station is nearest to the Atlanta Stadium?
4. Why is it important to be able to read transportation maps?

A Suburb in England

READ TO LEARN

■ Key Places

Richmond   London   England

■ Read Aloud

Last week Tiffany's class had a visitor from another country. His name is Kevin Bacon and he came from England. Tiffany wrote a story about him for the school newspaper. Before she wrote her story, she asked Kevin some questions.

■ Read for Purpose

1. **WHAT YOU KNOW:** What are three things you know about the country of England?
2. **WHAT YOU WILL LEARN:** How is Richmond like Austell?

Newspaper writers ask questions when they write a story. What questions would you ask someone from England?

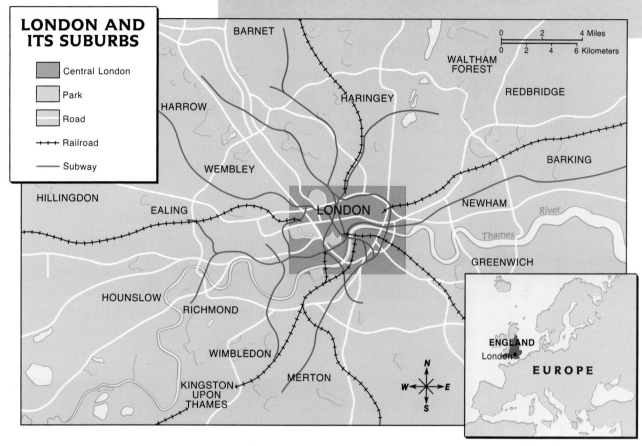

LONDON AND ITS SUBURBS

- ■ Central London
- ▢ Park
- ▢ Road
- ┼┼┼ Railroad
- ── Subway

BARNET

WALTHAM FOREST

REDBRIDGE

HARINGEY

HARROW

BARKING

WEMBLEY

HILLINGDON

EALING

LONDON

NEWHAM

River

Thames

GREENWICH

HOUNSLOW

RICHMOND

WIMBLEDON

ENGLAND
London

EUROPE

KINGSTON UPON THAMES

MERTON

0   2   4 Miles
0   2   4   6 Kilometers

A VISITOR FROM ENGLAND

TIFFANY: Kevin, what is the name of the place where you live?

KEVIN: It is called Richmond. It is a suburb of London. London is the largest city in England, and the capital of England.

TIFFANY: What makes your community a suburb?

KEVIN: Most people who live in Richmond work in London. They commute from Richmond to London every workday.

TIFFANY: Is Richmond like suburbs in the United States?

183

In London people use the subway, called the "tube," or double-decker buses to get to work.

KEVIN: In some ways it is. It has many shops and stores where people can buy the things they need. Most shops are like the stores you have here in Austell. But they have different names, like "petrol station" and "greengrocer."

TIFFANY: What is a petrol station and a greengrocer?

KEVIN: Americans call a petrol station a gas station. A greengrocer is a store that sells fruits and vegetables.

TIFFANY: How do commuters in Richmond get to their jobs in London?

KEVIN: We have good public transportation just like here. My father rides the "tube" to work. That's what we call a subway.

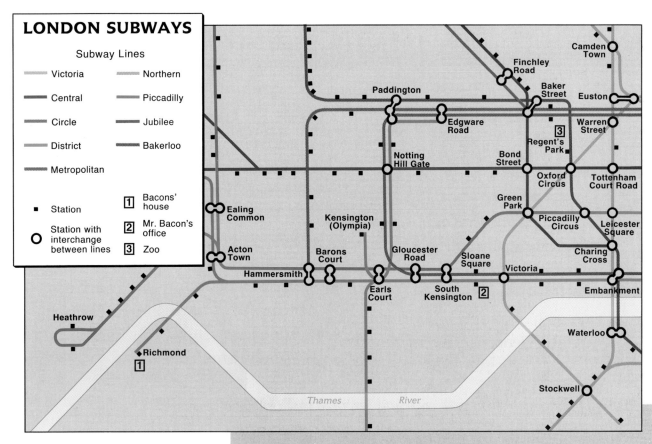

LONDON SUBWAYS

Subway Lines

— Victoria   — Northern

— Central   — Piccadilly

— Circle   — Jubilee

— District   — Bakerloo

— Metropolitan

■ Station

○ Station with interchange between lines

1 Bacons' house

2 Mr. Bacon's office

3 Zoo

MAP SKILL: This map shows part of London's subway system. Which subway line does Mr. Bacon take to go to work?

TIFFANY: What do you like best about living in Richmond?

KEVIN: It's quieter than London. We have a garden behind our house. It's nice to be close to London so we can go there often to see a play or to visit the zoo.

Check Your Reading

1. Why is Richmond a suburb?

2. Name three ways that Richmond is like Austell.

3. **THINKING SKILL:** How is your community like Richmond? How is it different?

IDEAS TO REMEMBER

- All suburbs depend on good transportation because the people who live in them often travel to work in a nearby city.
- Suburbs are less crowded than cities and have homes where people live and stores where they shop.
- Austell, Georgia, like most suburbs, has public transportation, stores, and houses.
- Like Austell, the suburb of Richmond, England, has houses, stores, and good public transportation.

REVIEWING VOCABULARY

commuter   subway

public   transportation
transportation

Number a sheet of paper from 1 to 5. Beside each number write the word or words from the list above that best completes the sentence. One word can be used more than once.

1. Buses, cars, and bicycles are examples of _____.
2. A _____ is a person who travels from a suburb into a city to work each day.
3. MARTA is an example of a _____ system.
4. An underground train is called a _____.
5. Fewer people need to drive cars to work if there is good _____, such as buses and trains.

REVIEWING FACTS

1. Name three ways in which all suburbs are alike.
2. How did Austell, Georgia, change from a small farming town to a suburb?
3. What are three things Tiffany likes about living in a suburb?
4. What is the difference between public and private transportation?
5. Name two ways in which Richmond, England, is like Austell, Georgia.

WRITING ABOUT MAIN IDEAS

1. **Writing an Interview:** Imagine that you are a reporter for a

school newspaper. Write five questions you would ask a classmate about life in your community.

2. **Writing a Speech:** Write a short speech telling your class why you think suburbs are or are not the best communities in which to live.

3. **Writing a Paragraph:** Write a paragraph telling about the importance of public transportation to people who live in suburbs.

BUILDING SKILLS: READING TRANSPORTATION MAPS

Use the transportation map on page 185 to answer these questions.

1. How can you use a transportation map to learn how to get from one place to another?

2. What is the name of the subway line shown in purple?

3. How many stops are there on the District Line from Richmond to Hammersmith?

4. How is a transportation map useful?

STUDYING YOUR COMMUNITY

In Chapter 9 you read about suburbs and the importance of good transportation systems. Find out about transportation in your community. Find the answers to the following questions. How do people get to work, school, and shopping? Is there public transportation in your community? If so, what kind? If not, should there be? How could transportation in your community be improved? Write a report on transportation using the information you have gathered.

REVIEWING VOCABULARY

capital	producer
commuter	rural area
consumer	suburb
factory	transportation
industry	urban area

Number a sheet of paper from 1 to 10. Beside each number write the word or term from the list above that matches the definition.

1. A person who buys products
2. A city and the suburbs that surround it
3. A person who travels each day into a city to work
4. The moving of people and products from place to place
5. The many businesses that make one product
6. An area where small communities are surrounded by forests or farms
7. A city where the leaders of a state or country meet and work
8. A building where goods are made
9. A person who makes goods
10. A community located near a big city

((≡▷ WRITING ABOUT THE UNIT

1. **Writing a Letter:** Choose a city or town that you would like to visit. Write a letter to the Chamber of Commerce to find out about places to see.
2. **Writing in a Travel Diary:** When people travel, they often write about their trip in a travel diary. Pretend you are visiting Seattle for three days. Write about your visit. Tell what you saw each day.

ACTIVITIES

1. **Making a Flow Chart:** Make a flow chart to show how a farm product is used to make a food you eat. For example, you could learn how apple juice is made. Look in the library for information or write to a company that makes the product.
2. **Working Together to Find Out About Other Countries:** Find out about life in a city in another country. Find pictures or draw pictures which show what life is like in this city.

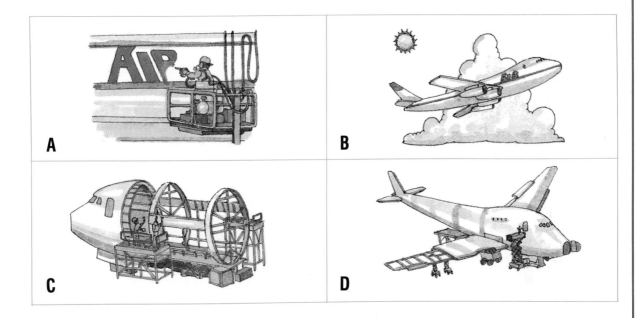

A

B

C

D

BUILDING SKILLS: SEQUENCING

Use the pictures above to answer these questions.

1. What do you do when you put things in sequence?
2. What kind of order can you use to put these pictures in sequence?
3. Which picture comes first?
4. Why is it important to know how to sequence?

 **LINKING PAST, PRESENT, AND FUTURE**

What kind of transportation might be invented in the future to make commuting into cities easier? Describe one invention you can imagine. Draw a picture that shows how it would work.

Pittsburgh 1800

Pittsburgh 1940

San Francisco 1990

San Francisco 1849

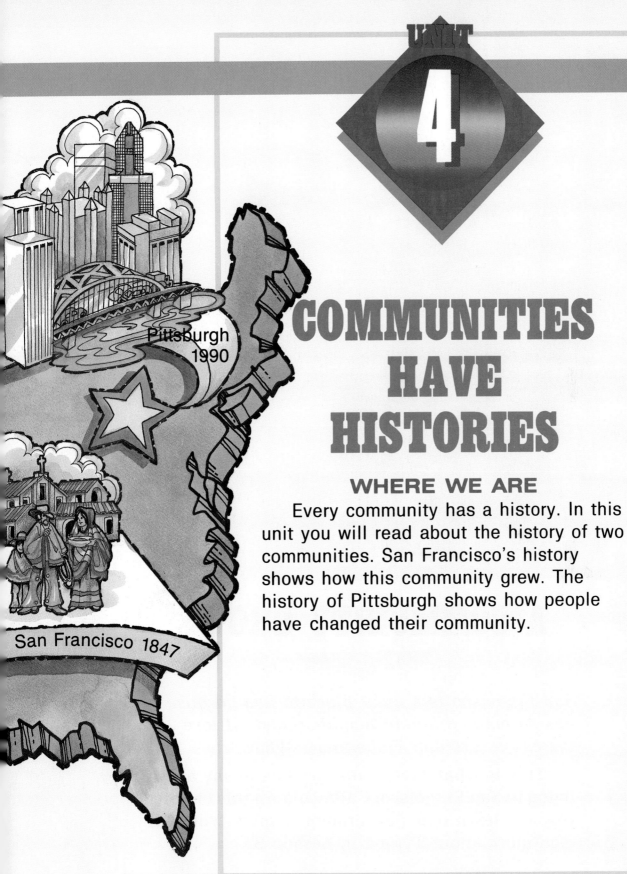

Pittsburgh
1990

San Francisco 1847

COMMUNITIES HAVE HISTORIES

WHERE WE ARE

Every community has a history. In this unit you will read about the history of two communities. San Francisco's history shows how this community grew. The history of Pittsburgh shows how people have changed their community.

CHAPTER 10

A COMMUNITY GROWS

FOCUS

San Francisco is a great place to live because it has so many different neighborhoods. I love the cable cars and Fisherman's Wharf.

This is what Tyrone Jue (jū) has to say about living in San Francisco, California. In this chapter you will learn how San Francisco grew. You will read more about Tyrone in Lesson 3.

1 The Geography of San Francisco

READ TO LEARN

Key Vocabulary

coast

Key Places

San Francisco
Golden Gate
San Francisco Bay
Pacific Ocean

Read Aloud

In 1987 the people of San Francisco held a birthday party for a bridge! The party was for the Golden Gate Bridge, which was 50 years old. To celebrate, the bridge was closed to all cars and trucks. Thousands of people paraded across it. Many more thousands wanted to join the parade, but the San Francisco police were afraid to let too many people on the bridge. They were afraid that the bridge might fall with so much weight on it.

Why did so many people want to celebrate a bridge's birthday? Bridges are important to the people of San Francisco. This lesson will help you understand why.

Read for Purpose

1. **WHAT YOU KNOW:** What bridge is located near your community?
2. **WHAT YOU WILL LEARN:** What is the geography of San Francisco like?

Thousands of people in San Francisco helped to celebrate the Golden Gate Bridge's birthday.

ON THE COAST

Find the Golden Gate Bridge on the map of San Francisco on this page. San Francisco is on the tip of a peninsula. The Golden Gate is to the north of the city, and San Francisco Bay is to the east. To the west of the city is the Pacific Ocean. The Golden Gate connects San Francisco Bay with the Pacific Ocean. San Francisco is located on the Pacific Coast. A coast is land next to an ocean. Because San Francisco is surrounded by water on three sides, bridges are important. Bridges connect San Francisco with suburbs and with other cities to the north and east.

San Francisco Bay is one of the largest natural harbors in the world. This has made San Francisco a very important port. Ships from all over the world can be found in the city's harbor.

MAP SKILL: San Francisco is located at the tip of a peninsula. What bridge connects San Francisco with cities and suburbs to the east?

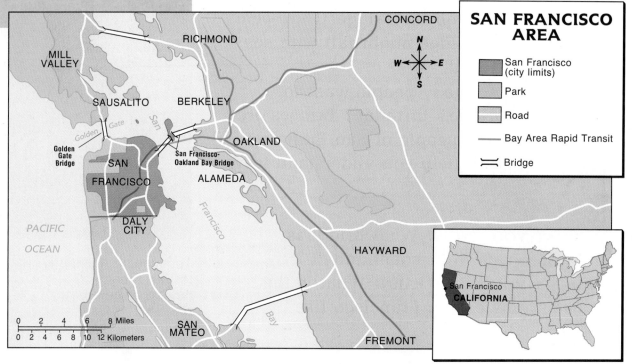

(*above*) Fog often covers the Golden Gate Bridge in the early morning. (*below*) There are more than 40 hills in San Francisco.

HILLS AND FOG

San Francisco's location also affects its climate. Being near the Pacific Ocean keeps San Francisco from getting too hot in the summer or too cold in the winter. But the city does get foggy. Early in the morning there are often huge clouds of fog.

Hills are an important feature of San Francisco's geography. The city has more than 40 hills. Some of these hills are so steep that the sidewalks have special steps to help people climb up and down them.

 Check Your Reading

1. Why are bridges important in San Francisco?
2. What is a coast?
3. **GEOGRAPHY SKILL:** Name three features of San Francisco's geography.
4. **THINKING SKILL:** How is the geography of San Francisco like the geography of your community? How is it different?

During the "gold rush," many people traveled to California on ships like the *Josephine*. These people hoped to find gold in California.

READ TO LEARN

■ Key Vocabulary

Forty-Niners

■ Read Aloud

In 1847 San Francisco was a small, quiet town with about 900 people. A visitor called it a "place with no business, no wealth, no power." Just three years later, San Francisco was a busy, booming city with more than 25,000 people. What changed San Francisco from a quiet town to a big city?

People caught gold fever. In 1848 gold was found about 100 miles (160 kilometers) northeast of San Francisco at a place called Sutter's Mill. Finding gold started the California "gold rush." By the following year, people from all over the country and other parts of the world began to travel to California in search of gold.

■ Read for Purpose

1. **WHAT YOU KNOW:** Describe San Francisco's geography.
2. **WHAT YOU WILL LEARN:** Why did San Francisco grow?

FORTY-NINERS

The people who came to California looking for gold were called "Forty-Niners" because the year was 1849. Many of the Forty-Niners came to California by ship. Their ships stopped in San Francisco because San Francisco was the port closest to the gold fields.

The trip by ship took a long time. From the east coast of the United States, it took about six months to sail to San Francisco. To pass the time at sea, passengers made up songs about the trip. A passenger from Massachusetts made up the song on the next page.

The Forty-Niners looked for gold in streams and dug for gold in the earth. Most of them never found any gold.

OH CALIFORNIA

(Oh Susanna)

Original Words and Music by Stephen Foster

Verse

I __ come from Sal - em Cit - y with my wash - bowl on my knee,

I'm __ going to Cal - i - for - nia the __ gold dust for to see;

It __ rained all day the day I left, the weath - er it was dry,

The __ sun so hot I froze to death, Oh broth - ers don't you cry.

Refrain

Oh Cal - i - for - nia... That's the land for me,

I'm __ bound for San Fran - cis - co with my wash - bowl on my knee.

A GROWING CITY

When the Forty-Niners reached San Francisco, they had to buy food, clothes, tools, and other supplies for gold hunting. Many new businesses were started in San Francisco to meet the needs of the gold miners. Many miners who did not find gold decided to stay in San Francisco. They liked San Francisco's beautiful location and mild climate. The city was growing.

But people in San Francisco had a problem—it was hard for people to get up and down the city's many hills. In 1873 cable cars were built to help solve this problem. Cable cars run on rails and are pulled by cables moving under the street. Riders could use the cable cars to go up and down San Francisco's high hills. This new kind of transportation helped people travel around San Francisco more easily.

Today you can still ride San Francisco's cable cars. You will read more about San Francisco today in the next lesson.

 Check Your Reading

1. Who were the "Forty-Niners"?
2. How did the California gold rush help San Francisco to grow?
3. **GEOGRAPHY SKILL:** How did geography affect San Francisco's history?
4. **THINKING SKILL:** What are two questions you could ask to find out more about cable cars?

Cable cars solved a transportation problem in San Francisco—how to go up and down the city's steep hills.

3 San Francisco Today

Meet Tyrone Jue. Tyrone enjoys playing basketball. He also likes visiting San Francisco's different neighborhoods.

READ TO LEARN

■ Key Vocabulary

immigrant

■ Key Places

Golden Gate Park
Embarcadero

■ Read Aloud

Tyrone Jue lives in San Francisco today. Tyrone thinks living in San Francisco is very exciting because there are so many places to visit. He also likes San Francisco because of its many neighborhoods. Many of these neighborhoods are home to people who came from other countries. Let's visit with Tyrone to learn about these neighborhoods and some of the special places to visit in San Francisco.

■ Read for Purpose

1. **WHAT YOU KNOW:** What are your favorite places to visit in your community?

2. **WHAT YOU WILL LEARN:** What are some special places to visit in San Francisco?

200

SAN FRANCISCO'S NEIGHBORHOODS

You can find some of San Francisco's neighborhoods on the map on this page. One of Tyrone's favorite places is his own neighborhood of Chinatown.

Many immigrants (im' ə grənts) from China came to San Francisco during the gold rush. An immigrant is a person who comes to live in a new country. More Chinese immigrants came later to help build the first railroad across our country.

"Immigrants also came to San Francisco from many other countries," says Tyrone. "Many immigrants from Italy live in the area of San Francisco called North Beach. The Mission District is home to many Spanish-speaking people. Many of the people who live there are the children and grandchildren of people from Mexico."

MAP SKILL: Chinatown is one of San Francisco's special neighborhoods. In what direction does Tyrone travel when he goes from Chinatown to Golden Gate Park?

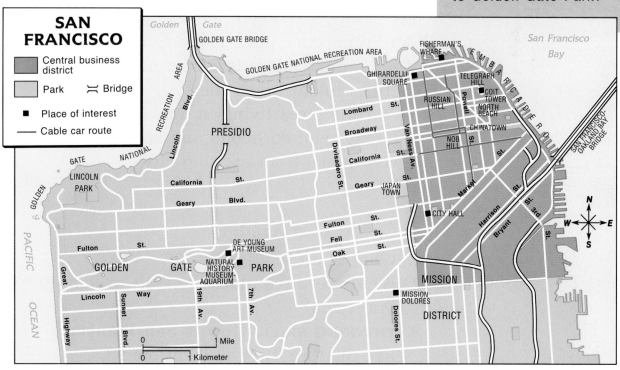

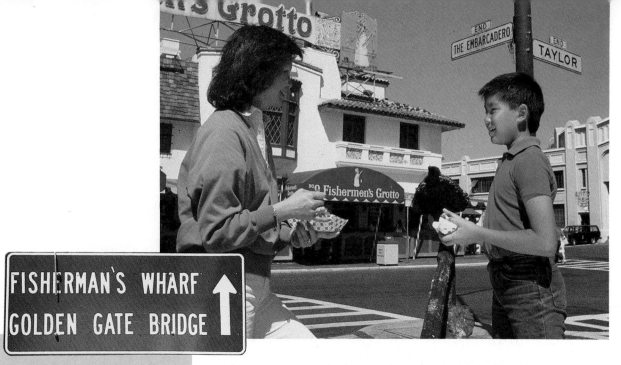

Tyrone and his mother like to eat seafood at Fisherman's Wharf.

SPECIAL PLACES IN SAN FRANCISCO

Tyrone enjoys visiting San Francisco's many beautiful parks. "Golden Gate Park is one of my favorites," says Tyrone. "From the western part of the park, I can look out over the Pacific Ocean."

Tyrone also likes riding a cable car to the Embarcadero (em bär kə de' rō). This is San Francisco's port. Tyrone's favorite part of the Embarcadero is Fisherman's Wharf. He likes to eat lunch there.

Tyrone loves living in San Francisco. Its different neighborhoods and special places to visit make it an exciting city.

Check Your Reading

1. What is an immigrant?
2. What are three places to visit in San Francisco?
3. **THINKING SKILL:** How is San Francisco like Seattle? How is it different?

A Growing Community in Kenya

READ TO LEARN

■ Key Places

Nairobi   Kenya   Mombasa

■ Read Aloud

Peter Roper and his family visited the city of Nairobi (nī rō′ bē) last summer. Nairobi is the capital of the country of Kenya. Kenya is on the east coast of the continent of Africa. Peter learned that Nairobi is like San Francisco because it is a growing city.

Now everyone in Peter's class wants to know about his visit to Nairobi. Here are the questions asked by Peter's classmates, and his answers.

■ Read for Purpose

1. **WHAT YOU KNOW:** What are two things you know about the continent of Africa?
2. **WHAT YOU WILL LEARN:** Why did the city of Nairobi grow?

(*above*) Peter Roper is an eight-year-old boy from San Francisco.
(*below*) Last summer he visited the city of Nairobi.

203

How did Nairobi begin?

Nairobi is about 90 years old. When Nairobi was built, Kenya was part of a colony ruled by England. The English were building a railroad across East Africa, starting from the coast on the Indian Ocean. Nairobi became a supply center for the railroad workers. Later, Nairobi became the capital of the colony. Today, Kenya is no longer a colony of England, but Nairobi is still its capital.

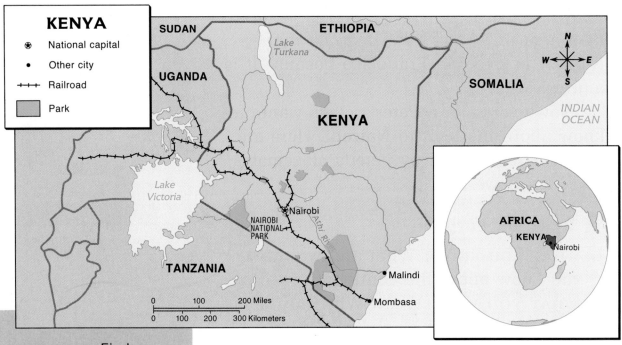

KENYA
- ⊛ National capital
- • Other city
- +++ Railroad
- ▨ Park

MAP SKILL: Find Nairobi on the map of Kenya. With which port city does the railroad connect Nairobi?

What helped the city grow?

After the railroad was built, Nairobi became a trading center. Goods came to the city by train from the port of Mombasa (mom bä' sə) on the coast. Farmers brought their crops to the city from the farms around Nairobi. Farmers traded crops for goods that

204

they needed. Trains carried some of the farmers' crops to markets in other parts of the country.

Is Nairobi still growing?

Yes, today the city is busier than ever. Now Nairobi is the main center for industry in Kenya. Making paper and cars are two important industries in Nairobi. Nairobi, like San Francisco, is a popular place for tourists to visit.

What did you like best about Nairobi?

I liked Nairobi National Park best. The animals are free to roam through the park. We traveled through the park in a big van with many windows. We saw zebras, leopards, and elephants.

 Check Your Reading

1. What helped Nairobi to grow?
2. How is Nairobi like San Francisco?
3. **GEOGRAPHY SKILL:** Look at the map on page 204. On what ocean is Kenya located?
4. **THINKING SKILL:** How is Nairobi like your own community? How is it different?

Kenya set up Nairobi National Park to help protect wild animals. Visiting the park was the best part of Peter's trip.

Predicting

Predicting is telling what will happen next based on what you already know. To predict something, you must understand how one thing causes another thing to happen. For example, you may tell your little brother not to touch a stove because you know that he could burn himself.

Trying the Skill

Read the story about Tyrone. Then use the information to predict what is most likely to happen next.

Tyrone plays basketball on his community center's team. Last year each player on the team that won a championship received a trophy. This year, Tyrone's team won the championship. Which of the following is most likely to happen?

A. The team will have a party.
B. Each player will receive a trophy.
C. Nothing will happen.

How were you able to predict what would happen next?

HELPING YOURSELF

One Way to Predict	Example
1. Review the information you have been given.	Last year each player on the team that won the championship received a trophy.
2. Think of what you already know about the situation described.	Many team members receive trophies when they win a championship.
3. Look for a pattern in what you know that tells what will happen next.	Winning team members usually receive trophies.
4. Think of all that could happen.	This year Tyrone's team could (A) have a party, (B) receive trophies, (C) not do anything.
5. Choose what is most likely to happen next.	The team members will most likely receive trophies.

Applying the Skill

Read the story. Predict what Jim Brady will do.

Jim Brady left Boston to look for gold in California. He found none. Soon his money ran out. He liked San Francisco and knew it was a growing city. Will Brady sail back to Boston? Will he try to find a job in San Francisco?

Check yourself by answering the following questions.

1. When you predict, you tell
   a. everything that can happen.
   b. what will most likely happen.
   c. what has happened.
2. To predict what Jim Brady will do, you should think about
   a. how to find gold.
   b. why people stay in a place.
   c. how people travel from Boston to San Francisco.

Reviewing the Skill

1. What are some words that mean the same thing as *predicting*?
2. How can predicting the weather help you?

IMPORTANT EVENTS

1848
Gold is discovered near San Francisco

1879
Cable cars are invented

1987
The Golden Gate Bridge is 50 years old

1800

1900

IDEAS TO REMEMBER

- San Francisco is located on a peninsula on the Pacific Coast.
- San Francisco grew when Forty-Niners came to California looking for gold.
- Today San Francisco has many special neighborhoods and places to visit.
- Nairobi, like San Francisco, has grown to be a large city.

REVIEWING VOCABULARY

Number a sheet of paper from 1 to 5. Read the definition of each underlined word. Beside each number, write **T** if the definition is true and **F** if it is false.

1. The <u>Forty-Niners</u> were people who came to California in 1849 to look for gold.
2. A <u>coast</u> is high, flat land.
3. An <u>immigrant</u> is a person traveling on vacation.
4. A <u>coast</u> is land next to an ocean.
5. An <u>immigrant</u> is a person who comes to live in a new country.

REVIEWING FACTS

1. What are two features of San Francisco's geography?
2. What happened in 1848 that caused San Francisco to grow?
3. Why are cable cars important in San Francisco?

4. Name two neighborhoods in San Francisco that began as homes for immigrants.

5. How did the railroad help Nairobi to grow?

◖▱▷ WRITING ABOUT MAIN IDEAS

1. Writing a Letter: Pretend you are Tyrone Jue's pen pal. Write a letter to him. Tell him about ways that your community is like his. Also tell about ways that it is different.

2. Writing a Story: Look at the pictures of Forty-Niners on pages 196 and 197. Use the people in the pictures as characters in a story about the Gold Rush.

3. Making a Chart: Make a chart that compares and contrasts San Francisco and Nairobi. Make two columns on your chart. Label one column *San Francisco,* and the other *Nairobi.* Down the side of the chart list *Geography, History,* and *Interesting Sights.* Fill in the chart with information from the chapter.

BUILDING SKILLS: PREDICTING

1. What do you do when you predict?

2. Predict two things that you think will happen on your birthday. Tell why you think they will happen.

3. There is a rule in Tyrone's school to not run in the halls. What do you predict would happen if one of Tyrone's friends ran in the hall?

4. Why is it important to know how to predict?

STUDYING YOUR COMMUNITY

In 1987 the people in San Francisco celebrated the birthday of the Golden Gate Bridge. Choose an important place in your community. It might be a library, school, train station, or bridge. Find out when the place you have chosen was built. Also find out some important facts about it. Then plan a birthday party for the place. It should be a party for everyone in your community.

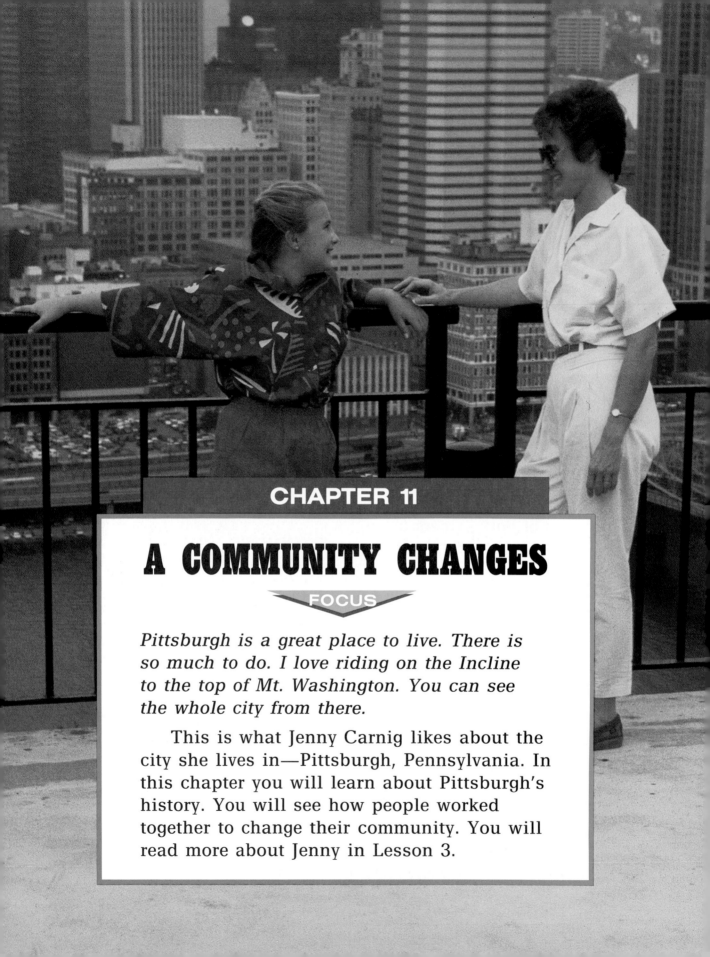

CHAPTER 11

A COMMUNITY CHANGES

FOCUS

Pittsburgh is a great place to live. There is so much to do. I love riding on the Incline to the top of Mt. Washington. You can see the whole city from there.

This is what Jenny Carnig likes about the city she lives in—Pittsburgh, Pennsylvania. In this chapter you will learn about Pittsburgh's history. You will see how people worked together to change their community. You will read more about Jenny in Lesson 3.

1 The Geography of Pittsburgh

READ TO LEARN

Key Vocabulary
fuel

Key Places
Pittsburgh

Read Aloud

Imagine that you are in an airplane flying high above the city of Pittsburgh, Pennsylvania. Far, far below you see a giant blue letter *Y*. As your airplane gets closer to the ground, you see that the blue *Y* is really water. You see many bridges crossing this water.

After your plane lands, you look at a map of Pittsburgh. The map shows you that the *Y* you saw is the three rivers that flow through Pittsburgh. The Allegheny (al ə gā′ nē) River and the Monongahela (mə nong gə hē′ lə) River, meet in the city to form the Ohio River.

Pittsburgh is located at the point where the Allegheny (*left*) and Monongahela (*right*) rivers meet to become the Ohio River.

Read for Purpose

1. **WHAT YOU KNOW:** Why are rivers important to communities?
2. **WHAT YOU WILL LEARN:** How did Pittsburgh's geography help it to grow?

211

A CENTER FOR TRADE

Look at the map of Pittsburgh below. Find the three rivers that are in Pittsburgh. Do you see how they form a *Y*? These three rivers helped Pittsburgh become an important port.

In the early 1800s many Americans began moving west. They often traveled by boat down the Ohio River. Their river trip started in Pittsburgh. Pittsburgh's location helped it become a center for trade and transportation for these travelers.

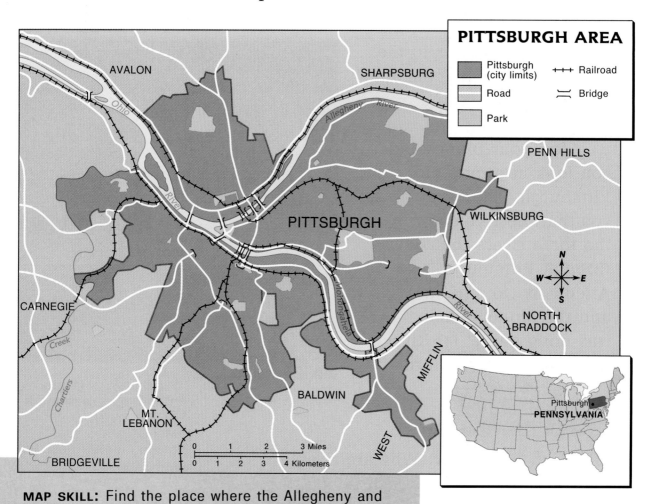

MAP SKILL: Find the place where the Allegheny and Monongahela rivers meet to form the Ohio River. Is this place inside or outside Pittsburgh's city limits?

212

(*left*) Steel is made in huge furnaces. (*below*) Miners dig the coal that is needed to make steel.

COAL AND STEEL

In the area all around Pittsburgh, miners found an important natural resource—coal. Coal is used as fuel (fū′ əl). A fuel is something that is burned to make heat or provide power. People use coal to heat their homes. Coal is also used to make electricity.

Coal helped Pittsburgh become the biggest producer of steel in the United States. Steel is a very hard metal made from iron. Steel is used to make things like cars and train rails. Iron must be heated to very hot temperatures to make steel. Coal is a good fuel for heating iron to make steel.

Pittsburgh never had a "coal rush." But resources did bring people to the city just as gold brought people to San Francisco.

 Check Your Reading

1. What is a fuel?
2. How is steel made and used?
3. **GEOGRAPHY SKILL:** How did Pittsburgh's resources help this city to grow?
4. **THINKING SKILL:** Predict what might have happened to Pittsburgh if coal had not been found nearby.

Reading Product Maps

Key Vocabulary
product map

You read that coal is an important resource in the area around Pittsburgh. Is coal found anywhere else in the state of Pennsylvania? You could find the answer to this question by looking at a product map. A product map shows where resources are found. It also shows where crops are grown and goods are manufactured.

Using a Product Map

The pictures below show you some of the products made or grown in Pennsylvania. Now look at the product map of Pennsylvania on the next page. The symbols on the map show you from where in Pennsylvania the products shown below come. The map key tells you what these symbols mean. What is the symbol for vegetables? What does the cow symbol stand for?

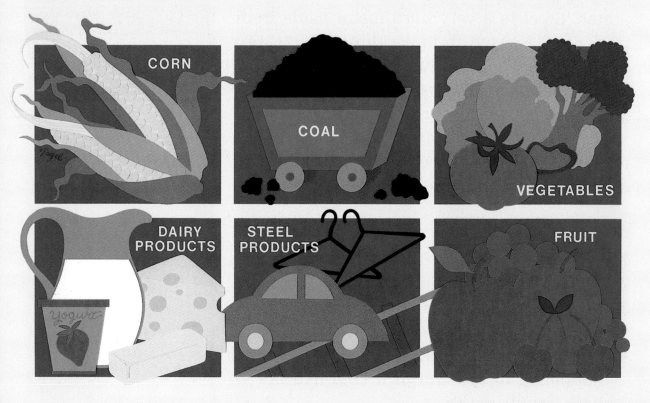

CORN

COAL

VEGETABLES

DAIRY PRODUCTS

STEEL PRODUCTS

FRUIT

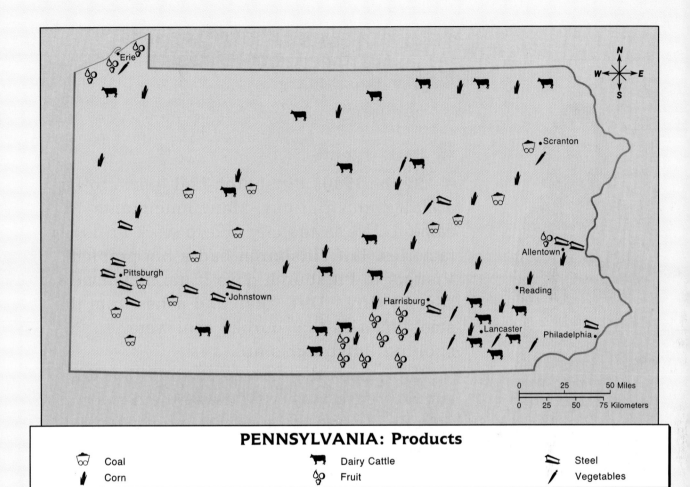

PENNSYLVANIA: Products

Coal			Dairy Cattle			Steel	
Corn			Fruit			Vegetables	

Look at the map to find the corn symbol near the city of Reading. It tells you that corn is grown near Reading. Near what other community is corn grown?

By looking at the symbols on the map, you can tell that Pittsburgh and Johnstown are located in areas where mining and manufacturing are important. You can also tell that farming is important near Lancaster and Harrisburg.

Reviewing the Skill

1. What is a product map?
2. Name two products that are grown in Pennsylvania.
3. What products are grown or raised near the city of Erie? Near Lancaster?
4. Why is it important to know how to read product maps?

215

2 Pittsburgh Changes

READ TO LEARN

■ Key Vocabulary

pollution

■ Read Aloud

By the 1940s Pittsburgh had grown to be a large industrial city. Many immigrants came to live in the city and to work in its factories. But Pittsburgh had a big problem. Visitors to Pittsburgh gave it the nickname "Smoky City." Dirt, dust, and ashes from the steel factories that burned coal were spoiling Pittsburgh's air.

Sometimes the air was so dirty that the city was dark in the middle of the day. Streetlights had to be turned on at noon. Smoke and ashes fell on houses, schools, and offices. It made them dark and dirty.

■ Read for Purpose

1. **WHAT YOU KNOW:** Why did Pittsburgh grow to be a large city?
2. **WHAT YOU WILL LEARN:** How did people change Pittsburgh?

Many immigrants came to work in the steel factories of Pittsburgh and in the coal mines nearby.

The Granger Collection

216

POLLUTION

Pittsburgh had a terrible pollution problem. Pollution is dirt that spoils land, water, or air. People in Pittsburgh were worried about the pollution. They were tired of hearing their city called the "Smoky City."

Leaders of the city decided to start a clean-up program. They asked the owners of factories to put equipment in their factories that would take some of the dirt from the smoke when coal was burned.

Getting factory owners to agree to the new rules on pollution was not easy. The equipment needed for the clean-up cost a lot of money. But little by little, everyone began to cooperate. The air in Pittsburgh got cleaner.

A "LIVABLE" CITY

Cleaning the air was just one step in changing Pittsburgh. City leaders also wanted to tear down some of the city's older buildings and clean and repair others. Many

(*bottom*) Many people worked in the factories in Pittsburgh. (*top*) But the factories also caused pollution.

people cooperated to make the project successful. Business leaders worked with city leaders to build a sports center. Many beautiful old buildings were repaired. Tall, modern buildings were also built.

After the people in Pittsburgh worked together to change their city, a writer thought of a new name for Pittsburgh. He called it "the most livable city in the United States." Pittsburgh has cleaner air and water, good schools and hospitals, and interesting places to visit. People in Pittsburgh expect their city to keep its new name for a long time.

Pittsburgh has solved its pollution problem. Today it is a clean and beautiful city.

Check Your Reading

1. What is pollution?
2. How did people in Pittsburgh work together to change their city?
3. **GEOGRAPHY SKILL:** How did the geography of Pittsburgh affect the city's history?
4. **THINKING SKILL:** How is Pittsburgh like your community? How is it different?

CLEANING UP
POLLUTION

When the people of Pittsburgh worked together to clean up their air and water, they set a good example. People in other towns and cities decided they could stop pollution too.

Marion Stoddart of Groton, Massachusetts, decided to try to clean up the river in her community. The Nashua River flows through her town. For years the river was so full of pollution

that people said it was "too thick to pour, but too thin to plow." People could smell the Nashua River from miles away.

Marion decided that the river had to be saved, and she spent 20 years doing it. At first people thought she was crazy. Her daughter remembers that some of her friends joked about her mother.

But Marion got people from towns all along the Nashua River to work together to clean up the river. Even the paper companies along the river, like the steel factories of Pittsburgh, realized that stopping pollution made good sense.

Thanks to Marion and her friends, fish and animals have returned to the Nashua River. People can use the beautiful public parks along the river.

In 1987 a group at the United Nations gave Marion a special honor. The group honored 90 people from throughout the world who had helped to protect the earth's resources. Marion was one of the people chosen to be honored. Marion's work has made her community a better place in which to live.

3 Pittsburgh Today

Jenny and her mother visit one of Pittsburgh's new buildings—the PPG Building.

READ TO LEARN

■ Key People

Andrew Carnegie

■ Read Aloud

Pittsburgh today mixes the old and the new. That is why Jenny Carnig likes living in Pittsburgh so much. Jenny is eight years old. She thinks Pittsburgh has changed in a special way. The air is clean and the buildings are new and modern. Yet all around the city there are reminders of Pittsburgh's past. There are buildings and museums that tell about the city's past.

Let's join Jenny as she visits some of the special places in her community.

■ Read for Purpose

1. **WHAT YOU KNOW:** What things in your community remind you of its history?
2. **WHAT YOU WILL LEARN:** How does Pittsburgh mix the old and the new?

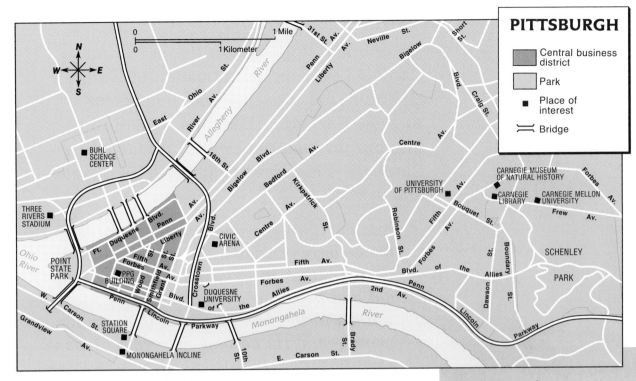

THE OLD AND NEW

Jenny starts her tour with a trip on the Monongahela Incline. The Incline is like the cable cars in San Francisco. It is over 100 years old. It takes people to the top of Mt. Washington, one of the highest hills in Pittsburgh. Many people use the Incline to commute to their jobs. The Incline is a reminder of the past that meets transportation needs in the present.

Station Square is another place where old and new come together in Pittsburgh. This huge building was once a busy railroad station. When the railroad closed, the station was no longer needed. Instead of tearing down Station Square, the people of Pittsburgh cleaned up the building. Today, many tourists visit Station Square.

MAP SKILL: Jenny likes to ride on the Monongahela Incline. On what street is the Monongahela Incline located?

ANDREW CARNEGIE

Another stop on Jenny's tour is the Carnegie (kär nā′ gē) Museum of Natural History. This museum was named for Andrew Carnegie. Like most people in Pittsburgh, Jenny knows all about Andrew Carnegie. This is what Jenny tells people about him.

Andrew Carnegie was an immigrant from the country of Scotland. He came to the United States in 1848 when he was 13 years old and began to work in a factory. He worked in the iron and steel industry for many years. He became an owner of many steel factories. People called him the "Steel King." By the time he was 60, he was one of the richest people in the world. Then he did something very special. He gave his money away.

Pittsburgh built the Carnegie Museum of Natural History (*right*) with money from Andrew Carnegie (*top*).

One way Andrew Carnegie used his money was to start public libraries in communities all over our country. He also gave money to Pittsburgh to build many libraries, schools, and museums like the Carnegie Museum of Natural History.

Jenny is proud of her community. She says it is "just right." When the people of Pittsburgh changed their city, they did not forget about their community's history.

The dinosaurs are Jenny's favorite part of the Carnegie Museum of Natural History.

 Check Your Reading

1. Why do most people in Pittsburgh know who Andrew Carnegie was?
2. What are two ways Pittsburgh mixes the old and the new?
3. **GEOGRAPHY SKILL:** Look at the map on page 221. Name a place of interest located in the central business district.
4. **THINKING SKILL:** How is Pittsburgh like San Francisco? How is it different?

A Changing Community in China

MAP SKILL: Daniel's aunt and uncle visited Beijing. Is the Forbidden City north or south of Tian An Men Square?

READ TO LEARN

■ Key Places

Beijing   China

■ Read Aloud

Daniel Diaz has a collection of post cards. His favorite post cards are from his aunt and uncle who visited Beijing (bā' jīng) in China. The post cards Daniel received help to show how Beijing has changed. You can find the places named in this lesson on the map below.

■ Read for Purpose

1. **WHAT YOU KNOW:** What are other things people collect?
2. **WHAT YOU WILL LEARN:** How has the city of Beijing changed?

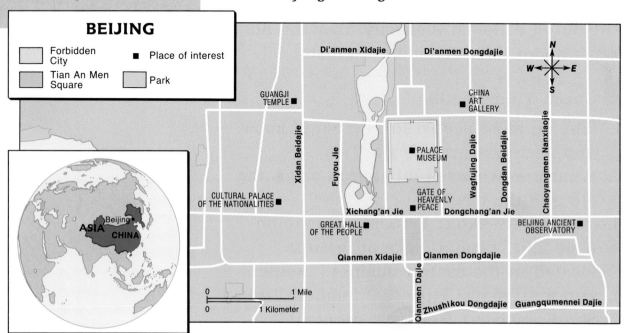

BEIJING

- ☐ Forbidden City
- ☐ Tian An Men Square
- ■ Place of interest
- ☐ Park

Di'anmen Xidajie   Di'anmen Dongdajie

GUANGJI TEMPLE ■

CHINA ART GALLERY ■

CULTURAL PALACE OF THE NATIONALITIES ■

■ PALACE MUSEUM

Xidan Beidajie

Fuyou Jie

Wagtujing Dajie

Dongdan Beidajie

Chaoyangmen Nanxiaojie

GATE OF HEAVENLY PEACE ■

Xichang'an Jie   Dongchang'an Jie

GREAT HALL OF THE PEOPLE ■

BEIJING ANCIENT OBSERVATORY ■

ASIA   Beijing
CHINA

Qianmen Xidajie   Qianmen Dongdajie

Qianmen Dajie

0   1 Mile
0   1 Kilometer

Zhushikou Dongdajie   Guangqumennei Dajie

224

Dear Daniel,

We have just arrived in Beijing, China. Beijing used to be called Peking. Beijing is a very old city, but it has also changed in many ways. This post card shows one of the oldest parts of Beijing. This is where the Chinese emperor, or ruler, used to live. This part of the city is called the Forbidden City because at one time people could only enter it with the emperor's permission.

But today, all of that has changed. China is no longer ruled by an emperor. Now millions of people visit the Forbidden City every year to enjoy its parks and museums. Aunt Paula says hello.

Uncle Harold

225

Dear Daniel,

This is the Gate of Heavenly Peace on Tian An Men Square. This is one of the most famous places in Beijing. The gate was built a long time ago. There are also many modern buildings on this square. One of these modern buildings is called the Great Hall of the People. This is where China's leaders meet today. Your Uncle Harold and I enjoyed visiting Tian An Men Square.

Aunt Paula

Dear Daniel,

Our tour bus went past long blocks of apartment buildings like the ones you see in this post card. Many of Beijing's old walls and gates were torn down to make way for these apartments. Beijing needs many large apartment buildings like these because the city is growing. People have come to live in Beijing and to work in its industries. Modern buildings like these are one important way Beijing has changed. Aunt Paula and I can't wait to see you!

Uncle Harold

Check Your Reading

1. What is the Forbidden City?
2. How has Beijing changed?
3. **THINKING SKILL:** How is Beijing like Pittsburgh? How is it different?

227

IMPORTANT EVENTS

1800
Pittsburgh becomes a trade and transportation center

1940s
Smoke from factories pollutes Pittsburgh

1990
Pittsburgh is a clean, livable city

1800

1900

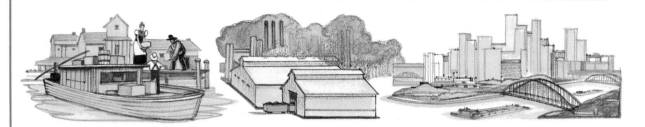

PEOPLE TO KNOW

Andrew Carnegie (1835–1919)

IDEAS TO REMEMBER

- Pittsburgh's river location and coal resources helped it to grow.
- People in Pittsburgh worked together to stop pollution from spoiling their city.
- Today Pittsburgh is a beautiful, clean city that has mixed the old and the new.
- Beijing, like Pittsburgh, is both an old and a new city.

REVIEWING VOCABULARY

fuel   pollution

Number a sheet of paper from 1 to 5. Beside each number write the word from the list above that best completes each sentence. The words can be used more than once.

1. Smoke from factories can cause _____.
2. Coal is a _____ used for heating iron to make steel.
3. _____ is dirt that spoils the land, the water, or the air.
4. A _____ is burned to make heat or provide power.
5. Air _____ can be caused by dirty smoke from factories.

REVIEWING FACTS

1. Name two of Pittsburgh's natural resources.
2. Why was Pittsburgh once called the "Smoky City"? Why is it not called that today?
3. Name two ways Andrew Carnegie helped Pittsburgh.
4. What are three interesting places in Pittsburgh?
5. Give one example of how Beijing has mixed the old and the new.

✎ WRITING ABOUT MAIN IDEAS

1. **Writing a Report:** Write a report telling how coal has been both good and bad for Pittsburgh.
2. **Writing a Paragraph About Geography:** Write a paragraph that answers the following question: "Why do you think Pittsburgh's new sports center is called Three Rivers Stadium?"
3. **Writing an Interview:** Imagine that you could meet Andrew Carnegie. What would you ask him? Write at least three questions you would ask.

BUILDING SKILLS: READING PRODUCT MAPS

Use the product map on page 215 to answer these questions.

1. If you wanted to find out where coal is found in Pennsylvania, how would a product map help you?
2. Near what two cities might a person see vegetable farms?
3. What symbol stands for steel?
4. Name one place where steel is made.
5. Why is it important to know how to read product maps?

STUDYING YOUR COMMUNITY

Some people call Pittsburgh "the most livable city in the United States." Chicago, Illinois, is known as the "Windy City." Denver, Colorado, is sometimes called the "Mile-High City." These nicknames come from the best or most interesting feature of each city. What would be a good nickname for your community? If it already has a nickname, what other name could you give it?

REVIEWING VOCABULARY

coast   immigrant
Forty-Niners   pollution
fuel

Number a sheet of paper from 1 to 5. Beside each number write the word or term from the list that matches the definition.

1. A person who moves from one country to live in another country
2. People who went to California in search of gold in 1849
3. Something that is burned to make heat or power
4. Dirt that spoils land, water, or air
5. Land next to an ocean

◀◼▶ WRITING ABOUT THE UNIT

1. **Writing a Diary Entry:** Look at the picture of a cable car on page 195, and at the one of the Monongahela Incline on page 221. Imagine you had a chance to ride on either the cable car or the Incline. Write a diary entry about your ride.

2. **Writing a Letter to the Editor:** Suppose that you lived in Pittsburgh in the 1940s when pollution was a problem. Write a letter to the editor of the city newspaper. In your letter tell your ideas about how and why the factory owners should cooperate to help clean up pollution.

ACTIVITIES

1. **Researching Places in Beijing:** Find out more about one of the places you read about in the lesson on Beijing. You could choose the Forbidden City, for example. Find out about the place's history and who goes there or uses it today. Then write a report.

2. **Working Together to Make Posters:** Work together as a class to make two posters that tell about China and Kenya. Put labels and pictures on them that show each country's flag, the special clothes people in each place wear, and the special customs these people follow.

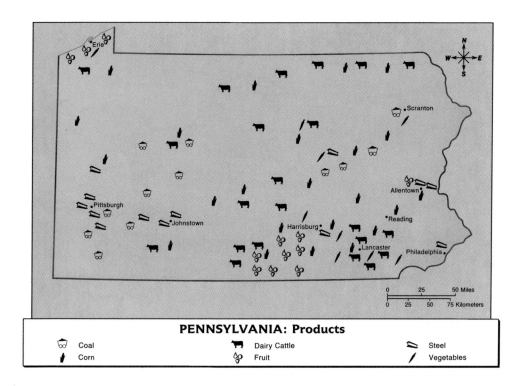

PENNSYLVANIA: Products

 Coal		Dairy Cattle		Steel	
Corn		Fruit		Vegetables	

BUILDING SKILLS:
READING PRODUCT MAPS

Use the map to answer the following questions.

1. How do you read a product map?
2. What is the symbol for coal?
3. Name two products that come from the northwestern part of Pennsylvania.
4. Why is it useful to know how to read product maps?

LINKING PAST, PRESENT, AND FUTURE

Find out how your community began by getting information from your library. Then decide how you would like your community to be in the future. Tell what changes you would like to see.

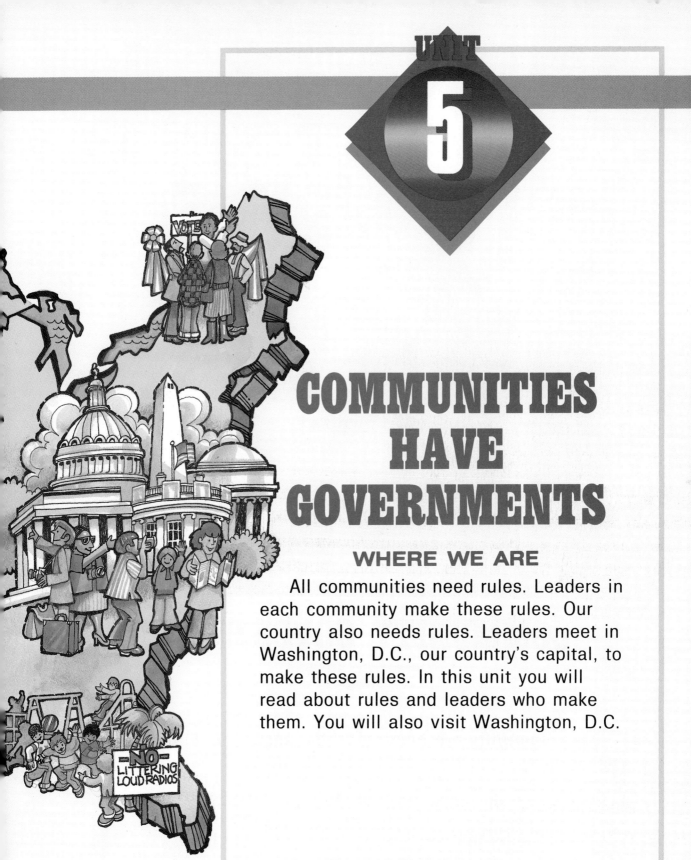

5

COMMUNITIES HAVE GOVERNMENTS

WHERE WE ARE

All communities need rules. Leaders in each community make these rules. Our country also needs rules. Leaders meet in Washington, D.C., our country's capital, to make these rules. In this unit you will read about rules and leaders who make them. You will also visit Washington, D.C.

CHAPTER 12

COMMUNITY GOVERNMENT

FOCUS

Two of the things I like best about living in my community are playing on the soccer team and being a member of Muncie Clean City.

Chris Taylor lives in Muncie, Indiana. In this chapter you will read about Chris, and learn how he helps his community. You will also learn about important community leaders and laws.

1 Communities and Rules

READc TO LEARN

▍ Key Vocabulary

law
vote

property
election

government

▍ Read Aloud

Every family has rules. In Chris Taylor's house there are rules about using the telephone and the television. There are rules about using other people's toys and about keeping the house clean. These rules help the Taylor family make decisions and solve problems.

Chris Taylor's school also has rules. There are rules about how children should act in the classroom and in the halls. Schools also have rules about what time school begins and ends.

Rules are also important in communities. In this lesson, you will learn about some of the rules in Chris's community of Muncie, Indiana.

▍ Read for Purpose

1. **WHAT YOU KNOW:** What are some rules in your house and your school?
2. **WHAT YOU WILL LEARN:** Why do communities need laws?

Chris and his family have rules about keeping their house clean. Chris helps by vacuuming.

235

COMMUNITY RULES

Rules for a community are called laws. Everyone must obey the laws. People who break laws can be punished.

Laws help to protect people. There are traffic laws which tell people how fast they can drive, and where they should stop. This helps keep people safe. Laws also protect property. Property is anything that people own. Houses and furniture are examples of property. Communities have laws about stealing a person's property. A person who steals usually has to go to jail.

Communities also have laws about public property. Public property is shared by all the people in the community. Parks and roads are both public property. In most communities there are laws about littering that help keep these places clean. What laws does your community have to help protect public property?

Many communities have signs like these. They tell about some of the laws in the community.

GOVERNMENT

Laws are made by the government. A government is a group of people who lead a community, a state, or a country. The leaders of a government also make sure laws are obeyed.

How do we choose our government leaders? In the United States we choose, or vote, for the people who run our government. We vote in an election. There are elections for government leaders of the community, state, and country. In the next lesson you will read about the community government of Muncie, Indiana.

In the United States the people choose government leaders by voting in elections.

✔ Check Your Reading

1. Why do communities have laws and government?
2. How are government leaders chosen?
3. **THINKING SKILL:** Name a government leader in your community.

237

Making Decisions

Every day you make many choices. You choose what clothes to wear. You choose what book you want to read. You choose a friend to invite to your house. You choose what you want to do after school. When you make these choices, you are making decisions.

To make a good decision you have to look at the possible choices you could make and then select the best one.

Trying the Skill

Suppose you and your friends want to play baseball in the park. Look at the picture below. Read the sign that is shown posted at the park entrance. Then answer the questions.

1. What are your choices of places to play in the park?
2. Which one is the best choice?
3. What did you do to make this decision?

COLUMBUS PARK

NO RUNNING ON PLAYGROUND.

NO DOGS ON FIELD.

NO BIKE RIDING ON BASKETBALL COURT.

One Way to Make Decisions	Example
1. Tell what it is you want to do.	You want to play baseball.
2. Think about all the choices you have.	You could play on the playground, basketball court, or field.
3. Think about the possible outcomes of the choices.	For example, playing on the playground would break a rule.
4. Decide what is good about each choice.	For example, there is lots of room to play on the field.
5. Decide which choice is the best.	So, playing on the field is the best choice.

Applying the Skill

Sally Wong wants to be a volunteer in her community. She is a third-grader and she likes to be outdoors. Look at the list below. Which job should she choose?

Volunteers Needed!

1. Serve meals to the homeless.
2. Help out at the day-care center.
3. Clean up leaves in the park.
4. Help out at the Senior Citizens Center.

1. To make a decision Sally should
   a. choose any job on the list.
   b. think about the outcome of each choice.
   c. ask her friends what to do.
2. Since Sally wants to work outdoors, she should choose
   a. Job 1
   b. Job 3
   c. Job 4

Reviewing the Skill

1. What is one way you could follow to make a decision?
2. Give an example of a decision you made today.
3. Why is it important to be able to make decisions?

2 A Community's Government

Chris Taylor's father wanted to win a community election. He met with many people to ask them to vote for him.

READ TO LEARN

◼ Key Vocabulary

city council
mayor
tax

◼ Key Places

Muncie, Indiana

◼ Read Aloud

On election night about ten years ago, Chris Taylor's father got some bad news. He had tried very hard to get elected to the government of his city. He had made over 20 speeches telling voters why he thought he was the best person for the job. He hoped the voters would agree. On election night Mr. Taylor learned that he had lost the election.

Today Mr. Taylor says that losing the election was good for him. "It made me work even harder to meet the people of my community to tell them my ideas about government," he said. Four years later he ran for city government again. This time Mr. Taylor won.

◼ Read for Purpose

1. **WHAT YOU KNOW:** Why are elections important?
2. **WHAT YOU WILL LEARN:** What are the responsibilities of a mayor and a city council?

COUNCIL AND MAYOR

Mr. Taylor was elected to be a member of the city council of Muncie, Indiana. A city council is a group of elected people who make laws for a community. Most communities have a city council to make needed laws.

Muncie, like most communities, also has a mayor. A mayor is elected by the people of a community to make sure laws are obeyed. The mayor also chooses people to help run the community, like the police chief and the fire chief.

Chris Taylor's father and the other members of the Muncie City Council meet once a month. At these meetings the council talks about many kinds of problems. They make decisions about where stoplights and stop signs should go. They listen to people who want more services or new roads near their homes.

Mr. Taylor and other members of the Muncie City Council meet once a month.

TAXES

An important job of the city council is to decide how the community's money should be spent. Community services cost money. People pay for the services in their community with taxes. A tax is money that people pay to support their government. Taxes help communities build libraries, roads, and schools. Money from taxes pays for community workers like police officers, firefighters, and sanitation workers.

Check Your Reading

1. How do the mayor and the city council lead a community?
2. Why are taxes important?
3. **THINKING SKILL:** Predict what might happen if people in a community did not pay taxes.

3 Being a Good Citizen

READ TO LEARN

Key Vocabulary

volunteer   citizen

Read Aloud

The leaders of Muncie invite Chris and his friends to march in a parade each year. They have earned a place in the parade by working to make their community a better place to live. Let's see how Chris and his friends have helped Muncie.

Chris and his friends are getting ready to march in a parade. They will carry brooms in the parade.

Read for Purpose

1. **WHAT YOU KNOW:** What is the group of government leaders called in most communities?

2. **WHAT YOU WILL LEARN:** How can people be good citizens?

Volunteers play an important role in community life. These volunteers are helping at a hospital.

COMMUNITY VOLUNTEERS

Chris and his friends are members of a group called Muncie Clean City. They are volunteers. This means they do not get paid for the work they do. This group works together to help keep Muncie clean. Once a year, Muncie Clean City volunteers get people to help them clean up all the litter along the White River, which runs through the middle of Muncie.

What kinds of volunteer groups does your community have? Many communities have volunteer ambulance drivers or firefighters. There are even volunteers who entertain children in the hospital. Volunteers are important to every community.

BEING A GOOD CITIZEN

When people are volunteers they are being good citizens (sit′ ə zənz). A citizen is a member of a community like Muncie and a member of a country like the United States.

How else can people be good citizens? You are being a good citizen when you help others and when you obey the laws. For citizens 18 years of age and older, voting in elections is another way to be a good citizen.

Mr. Taylor once gave a speech at Chris's school. A student asked him why he wanted to be in city government. This was his answer.

I think everyone should try to make their community a better place to live. I think I can do this by being on the city council. Helping other people through volunteer work is another way. Everyone can be a good citizen by obeying community laws.

One way to be a good citizen is to obey the laws. What law are these children obeying?

Check Your Reading

1. What is a volunteer?
2. What are three ways to be a good citizen?
3. **THINKING SKILL:** What are three questions you could ask to find out about the government of your community?

245

Should Girls Play Little League Baseball?

In this chapter you read about rules and laws. When people make rules and laws, they try to be fair. But sometimes rules and laws stop people from doing what they want.

Little League baseball has rules. One of its rules said that the Little League teams were for boys. In 1974, an 11-year-old girl from New Jersey decided this rule was not fair. She wanted the right to play Little League baseball. Soon girls in other places were trying to play on Little League teams.

Many people felt girls should not play on these teams. Others felt girls should be allowed to play. Here are some of the reasons both sides gave.

POINT

Girls Should Play Little League Baseball

Congresswoman Martha Griffiths of Michigan was one person who felt that girls have a right to play in the Little League. She said, "Sports are important. Girls should have a chance to compete with boys." Others in favor said, "If a girl has the skill she should be able to play." They felt that boys were not always stronger or faster than girls. They pointed out that boys playing Little League baseball were not equal in height, weight, or strength. Many girls were as fast and as strong as boys.

● How did Congresswoman Griffiths feel about girls playing Little League baseball?

COUNTERPOINT

Girls Should Not Play Little League Baseball

Those who said girls should not play in the Little League said that it was not safe. "Boys are stronger," they said. "Girls' bones are weaker and they run more slowly than boys." One Little League coach, Ray Platoni, warned, "We've had boys getting broken noses and chipped teeth. Girls will get hurt even more." Some gym teachers were afraid it might mean the end of girls' teams and girls' sports such as volleyball and softball. Others felt that boys would not feel comfortable playing with girls.

● Why did coach Ray Platoni believe girls should not be allowed to play Little League baseball?

UNDERSTANDING THE POINT/COUNTERPOINT

1. List the reasons given by people who wanted girls to play Little League baseball.
2. What were the reasons given by those who were against having girls play Little League baseball?
3. In your opinion, which side made the stronger case? Give your reasons.

IDEAS TO REMEMBER

■ Laws help to keep communities safe by protecting people and their property.

■ Most communities have a city council that makes the laws, and a mayor. The mayor chooses people to help run the community and makes sure the laws are obeyed.

■ People can be good citizens when they help other people in the community through volunteer work, and when they obey the laws.

REVIEWING VOCABULARY

citizen	mayor
city council	property
election	tax
government	volunteer
law	vote

Number a sheet of paper from 1 to 10. Beside each number write the word or term from the list above that matches each definition.

1. A group of elected people who make laws for a community
2. The voting that is held to choose government leaders
3. Anything that people own
4. A person who does not get paid for the work that he or she does
5. A leader elected by the people of a community to make sure laws are obeyed
6. The rules for a community
7. A group of people who lead a community, a state, or a country
8. To choose the people who run our government
9. A member of a community and of a country
10. Money that people pay to support their government

REVIEWING FACTS

1. Give two examples of a law that protects people.
2. What is the job of a city council?
3. What are two things for which tax money is used?
4. Name three jobs a volunteer might do.
5. How can people be good citizens?

✏️ WRITING ABOUT MAIN IDEAS

1. **Making a List:** List five classroom rules. Beside each one write how you think that rule helps solve problems in the classroom.

2. **Writing a Paragraph of Opinion:** Choose one law that you think is very important. Write a paragraph telling why you think the law is so important.

3. **Writing a Speech:** Write a brief speech telling your classmates why they should vote for you in an election for class president.

BUILDING SKILLS: MAKING DECISIONS

1. What are some ways you could follow to make a good decision?

2. Give an example of a decision you made today. What choices did you have? How did you decide on what choice to make?

3. Why is it important to be able to make good decisions?

STUDYING YOUR COMMUNITY

In Chapter 12 you read about community government. Find out about the government leaders in your community. Call the town or city hall in your community and find out who your leaders are. What job does each person do in the government? How long has he or she held the job? Make a chart naming each government leader, the job he or she holds, and what the job duties include.

If possible, invite one government leader to speak to your class. Before he or she arrives, be sure to prepare questions to ask the person.

CHAPTER 13

OUR COUNTRY'S CAPITAL

▼ FOCUS ▼

Washington, D.C., was a great place to visit. Visiting our capital helped me to learn about our country's government and its history.

This is how Christina Shorten described her visit to Washington, D.C., our country's capital city. In this chapter you will read about our country's history and its government. In Lesson 4 you will visit Washington, D.C., with Christina.

1 A New Country

READ TO LEARN

■ Key Vocabulary

American Revolution
Declaration of Independence

■ Key People

Thomas Jefferson

■ Key Places

Lexington, Massachusetts
Philadelphia, Pennsylvania

■ Read Aloud

A little over 200 years ago, our country was not a country at all. Parts of it were colonies ruled by governments in Europe. By 1750 England ruled 13 colonies along the coast near the Atlantic Ocean. But as the English colonies grew, so did the fights between England's leaders and the colonists.

This handmade blanket shows what a community in the American colonies looked like.

■ Read for Purpose

1. **WHAT YOU KNOW:** Name two communities in North America that began as colonies.
2. **WHAT YOU WILL LEARN:** Why did the English colonies decide to break away from England?

THE THIRTEEN ENGLISH COLONIES

MAP SKILL: This is a map of the 13 American colonies. Of what colony was Maine a part?

UNFAIR LAWS

Many colonists did not think England treated its American colonies fairly. By 1773 the English had passed laws making the colonists pay taxes on tea, glass, and other goods bought from England. The English government never asked the colonists how they felt about these taxes. Look at the song on the next page. The words tell how the colonists felt about the taxes.

Revolutionary Tea

Words by Seba Smith
Music by H. D. Munson

There was an old La-dy lived o-ver the sea, And

she was an Is - land Queen; __ Her daught-er lived off in a

new __ coun -trie, With an O-cean of wa-ter be - tween; __

The old la-dy's pock-ets were full __ of gold, But

nev-er con-tent-ed was she: __ So she called on her daught-er to

pay her a tax Of three pence a pound on her tea,

Of three pence a pound on her tea. __

The first shots of the American Revolution were fired in Lexington, Massachusetts.

THE WAR BEGINS

The English king sent soldiers to the colonies to be sure his laws were followed. In 1775 English soldiers and angry colonists fired at each other in Lexington, Massachusetts. These shots were the beginning of the war called the American Revolution. Colonists fought the American Revolution to make the colonies an independent, or free, country.

DECLARATION OF INDEPENDENCE

The leaders of the colonies met in Philadelphia, Pennsylvania, in the summer of 1776. They asked Thomas Jefferson to write to the English king explaining why the colonies wanted to be independent. Jefferson wrote the Declaration of Independence. On July 4, 1776, leaders of the colonies signed the Declaration of Independence. Many colonists were worried and afraid. They knew the Declaration meant they would have to fight a long war with England.

The colonists were also excited. The Declaration of Independence was the beginning of a new country. Today when we celebrate the Fourth of July, or Independence Day, we are remembering the birthday of our country.

Check Your Reading

1. What reason did the colonists have for wanting to break away from England?
2. Why did Thomas Jefferson write the Declaration of Independence?
3. **THINKING SKILL:** What are three questions you could ask to find out more about the American Revolution?

The **Declaration of Independence** was signed on July 4, 1776, in Philadelphia, Pennsylvania.

2 Governing Our Country

READ TO LEARN

Key Vocabulary

Constitution   President

Congress   Supreme Court

People welcomed the leaders of the new United States when they came to Philadelphia to plan our government.

Read Aloud

After the American Revolution, the 13 colonies became an independent country called the United States of America. The leaders of the new United States had a very important job to do. They had to decide what the government of our country would be like. They wanted to be sure the government was fair. The leaders of our country met to plan the new government and to decide on its laws.

Read for Purpose

1. **WHAT YOU KNOW:** What is the Declaration of Independence?
2. **WHAT YOU WILL LEARN:** How does the Constitution organize our government?

The Constitution, shown on the right, was written more than 200 years ago. Today people can see the Constitution when they visit Washington, D.C.

THE CONSTITUTION

In 1787 the leaders of our country met again in Philadelphia, Pennsylvania. This time they met to plan the way our new government would work. The plan they decided on is written in our Constitution. The Constitution contains all the most important laws for our country.

The Constitution divides our government into three parts, each with a different job. Each part of the government has the same amount of power.

OUR COUNTRY'S GOVERNMENT

Congress makes the laws for our country. People in every state elect lawmakers to serve in Congress.

Our country's leader is the President. The President makes sure all the laws in our country are carried out. The people in our country elect the President.

The Supreme Court is the country's most important court. There are nine judges on the Supreme Court. They judge the fairness of our country's laws. The judges of the Supreme Court are chosen by the President.

Congress, the President, and the Supreme Court are the three parts of our country's government.

George Bush was elected President of the United States in 1988.

Check Your Reading

1. Why is the Constitution so important?
2. What are the three parts of our government?
3. **THINKING SKILL:** How is Congress like a city council?

3 A Capital for a New Country

◼ Key People

George Washington
Benjamin Banneker
John Adams
Abigail Adams

◼ Key Places

Washington, D.C.

The Granger Collection

This is the place where the leaders of our country decided to build a new capital city.

◼ Read Aloud

It is a beautiful spot, capable of every improvement, and the more I view it, the more I am delighted with it.

This is how the wife of the first President to live in our capital described it. When Americans decided on a new government, they also had to decide on a new place for the country's capital. The leaders of the three parts of our government would work in this city. In this lesson you will read about our country's capital.

◼ Read for Purpose

1. **WHAT YOU KNOW:** What is the capital of the United States?
2. **WHAT YOU WILL LEARN:** What was Washington, D.C., like when it was first built?

Washington, D.C., was named for George Washington (*above*). Benjamin Banneker (*below*) helped to plan Washington, D.C. A stamp was made to honor him.

Benjamin Banneker

Black Heritage USA 15c

A NEW CAPITAL

Government leaders agreed that our country needed a new capital. But they had a hard time agreeing on where it should be located. You can read more about the decision on where to locate the new capital in the Point/Counterpoint on pages 262–263.

Our capital was named Washington, D.C., to honor George Washington. George Washington was our first President. He had led the Americans during the American Revolution.

PLANNING THE CAPITAL

President Washington asked a Frenchman named Pierre L'Enfant (pyer län' fän) to plan the new city. Before L'Enfant completed his planning of the city, he argued with other planners, and left. He took the plans for the new city with him. But Benjamin Banneker remembered all the plans. With Banneker's help, work on the capital soon began.

A CHANGING CITY

It was nine years before buildings in Washington, D.C., were ready. The first President to live in Washington, D.C., was John Adams. His wife, Abigail Adams, found life in this new city hard at first. Few people lived there. Streets were just mud tracks. In a letter to her daughter, she wrote, "Shiver, shiver, surrounded by forests, I have no wood for the fireplaces because people cannot be found to cut it."

Abigail Adams would find Washington, D.C., a very different place today. The wide streets are now filled with cars and buses. Underneath these streets, crowded subways carry thousands of government workers to and from their jobs each day. Many visitors come to Washington, D.C., each year.

Washington, D.C., has grown to become a large, modern city.

The Granger Collection

 Check Your Reading

1. Who was our first President?
2. How is Washington, D.C., different today from the way it was in 1800?
3. **THINKING SKILL:** Predict what might have happened if Benjamin Banneker did not remember the plans for Washington, D.C.

Where Should Our Capital Be Located?

The leaders of our country met in eight different cities during and after the American Revolution. When the Constitution was written in 1787 it called for a special place to be chosen as the capital of the United States. But the Constitution did not say where the capital should be built. For the next few years, the people in different parts of the country argued over where the capital should be.

The Capital Should Be in Philadelphia

The people of Pennsylvania wanted the capital in their state. They thought the city of Philadelphia would be a good place for the capital. One reason they thought Philadelphia was a good choice was because the Declaration of Independence had been signed there in 1776. Another reason was that Philadelphia was the largest city in the new country. It was also a busy port and an important center of trade.

As Northerners, the people of Pennsylvania did not want to see the capital in the South. They thought it would give too much power to the South.

● What was signed in Philadelphia in 1776?

The Capital Should Not Be in Philadelphia

Many people were against having the capital in a big city like Philadelphia. They were afraid that having the country's capital in a big city would make the new government weak. Southerners were afraid that the South would have less power if the capital were in the North.

The Constitution said that any land chosen for the new capital would have to be given to the country by the states. Virginia and Maryland offered some land to the country. The two states thought this land would be a good place for the capital because it was halfway between the North and the South.

● What two states offered land for the new capital?

UNDERSTANDING THE POINT/COUNTERPOINT

1. What are two reasons people wanted Philadelphia to be our country's capital?
2. Why was the South against having the capital in the North?
3. Which side do you think made the stronger case? Explain your answer.

Reading Grid Maps

Key Vocabulary
grid map

Imagine you are visiting a community for the first time. Think of how hard it would be to find your way around. One way to locate places in a community is to use a grid map. A grid map uses a grid, or a set of squares, to locate places on a map. You can also use a grid map to tell other people where places are located.

Locating Places
Each square on a grid map has two labels. One label is a number and the other label is a letter. The letters are shown along the left and right sides of the map. The numbers are shown along the top and bottom of the map.

Look at the grid map on the next page. It shows a community. The map key shows you what the symbols on the map stand for.

To use the grid, first find the pet store. Then slide your finger over to the left edge of the map. What letter do you come to?

Now put your finger back on the pet store. Then move it up to the top of the map. What number do you come to? The pet store is in **B-2**.

Now use the grid to find the school. The school is located in square **C-3**. First put a finger on the square labeled **C**. Now find the square labeled with the number **3** at the top of the map. Put a finger of your other hand on that square. Then move both fingers, one down and the other across, until they meet. They should meet at the square with the school in it.

Reviewing the Skill
Use the grid map to answer the following questions.
1. What is a grid map?
2. In what square is the lake located? What is located in square **D-4**?
3. Through what squares does Main Street run?
4. Why is it important to know how to use a grid map?

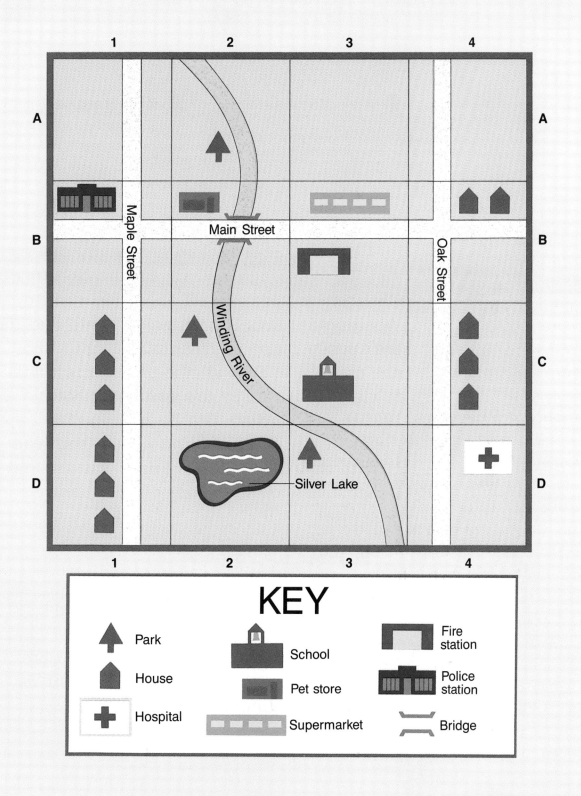

KEY

Park

House

Hospital

School

Pet store

Supermarket

Fire station

Police station

Bridge

4 A Tour of Washington, D.C.

READ TO LEARN

■ Key Vocabulary

Capitol
White House
monument

■ Key People

Abraham Lincoln

Christina uses a braille map to locate places in Washington, D.C.

■ Read Aloud

Christina Shorten and her family are visiting Washington, D.C., for the first time. Christina is very excited about her visit to Washington, D.C. Christina is blind, and there are special maps of Washington, D.C., that she can use to find all the places she wants to visit. These maps are written in both braille and English. Braille is a special way of writing that blind people can read with their hands. Let's join Christina and her family on their tour of our country's capital.

■ Read for Purpose

1. **WHAT YOU KNOW:** Why did our country's leaders decide to build Washington, D.C.?

2. **WHAT YOU WILL LEARN:** What are some important places to visit in Washington, D.C.?

THE CAPITOL AND THE WHITE HOUSE

You can find all the places the Shorten family visits on the map on pages 268–269. The first place they visit is the building where Congress meets. This building is called the Capitol. *Capitol*, the word for the building, sounds like *capital*, the word for the city. But, as you can see, these words are spelled differently.

After visiting the Capitol, Christina visits the White House. Every American President since John Adams has lived here. "At the White House, we visited five rooms that the President uses to entertain important guests," said Christina. "The rest of the rooms are not open to the public. The President lives and works in the other rooms."

In the Capitol, Christina is able to feel a statue of George Washington (*above*) and a copy of the Declaration of Independence (*below*).

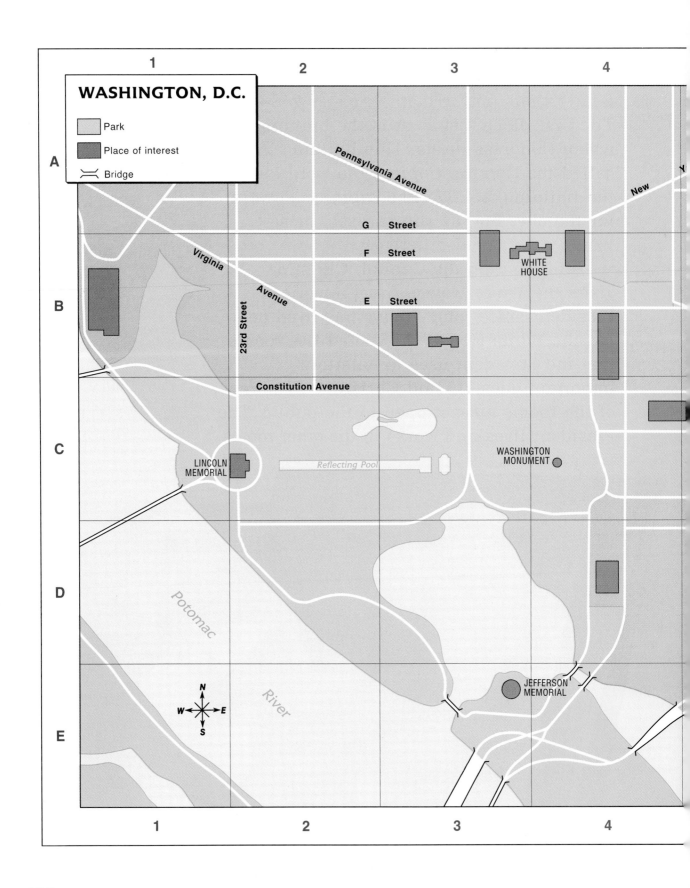

WASHINGTON, D.C.

Park

Place of interest

Bridge

Pennsylvania Avenue

New Y

G Street

F Street

WHITE HOUSE

Virginia Avenue

E Street

23rd Street

Constitution Avenue

LINCOLN MEMORIAL

Reflecting Pool

WASHINGTON MONUMENT

Potomac

River

N
W E
S

JEFFERSON MEMORIAL

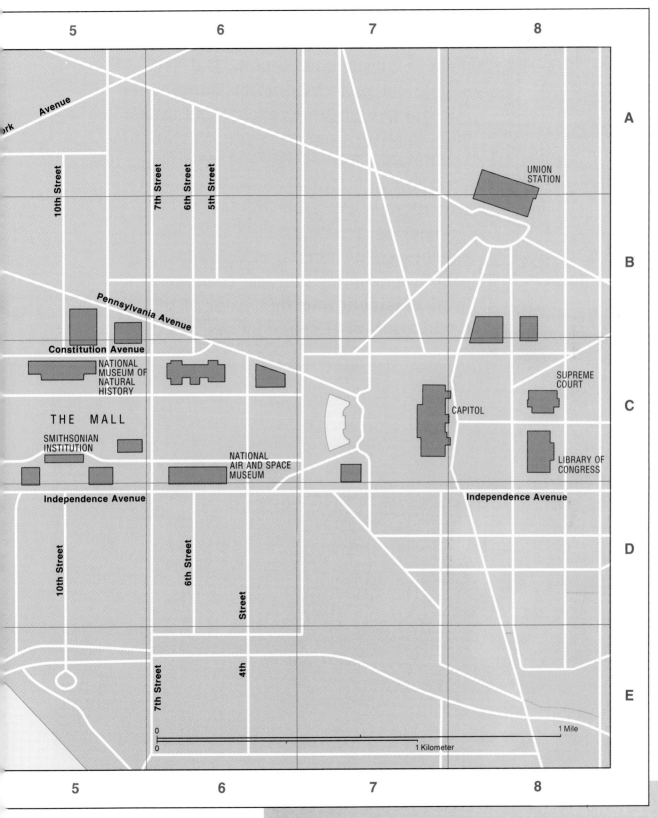

5 **6** **7** **8**

A

10th Street

7th Street
6th Street
5th Street

UNION STATION

B

Pennsylvania Avenue

Constitution Avenue

NATIONAL MUSEUM OF NATURAL HISTORY

SUPREME COURT

CAPITOL

C

THE MALL

SMITHSONIAN INSTITUTION

NATIONAL AIR AND SPACE MUSEUM

LIBRARY OF CONGRESS

Independence Avenue   Independence Avenue

D

10th Street

6th Street

Street

7th Street

4th

E

0
0   1 Mile
1 Kilometer

5 **6** **7** **8**

MAP SKILL: Christina began her tour of Washington, D.C., at the Capitol. In what grid is the Capitol located?

MONUMENTS

The Shorten family visits several monuments in Washington, D.C. A monument is a building or statue made to honor a person or an event. The tallest monument in the city is the Washington Monument. This is the first monument the Shortens visit. It was built to honor George Washington, our first President.

The Shortens also visit the Jefferson Memorial. The Jefferson Memorial helps people remember Thomas Jefferson, our third President and the writer of the Declaration of Independence.

(*left*) The Washington Monument was built to honor George Washington. (*right*) The Jefferson Memorial was built to honor Thomas Jefferson.

After visiting the Jefferson Memorial, the Shortens visit the Lincoln Memorial. The Lincoln Memorial was built to honor our 16th President, Abraham Lincoln. When Abraham Lincoln was elected President, most black people in our country were slaves. A slave is someone who is owned by another person. Lincoln helped to free the slaves.

Christina and her family felt proud of their country and its history after their visit to our capital. They hope to visit Washington, D.C., again soon.

SYMBOLS OF OUR COUNTRY

The monuments that Christina and her family visited in Washington, D.C., are important symbols of our country. Let's learn about another symbol of our country.

OUR COUNTRY'S FLAG

One of our country's most important symbols is our flag. The flag of the United States has 13 red and white stripes. These stripes stand for each of the 13 original colonies. The white stars on the flag stand for each of the 50 states that are part of our country today.

People show how important our flag is when they say the Pledge of Allegiance. Read the words in the Pledge of Allegiance on the next page.

When people say the Pledge of Allegiance they are honoring one of our country's most important symbols.

I pledge allegiance to the flag of the United States of America and to the Republic for which it stands, one Nation under God, indivisible, with liberty and justice for all.

When you "pledge allegiance" you promise to be loyal. Each time you say the Pledge of Allegiance, you are saying that you will be loyal to our country.

Visiting Washington, D.C., as Christina did, is a fun way to learn about being an American. Knowing about our country's symbols helps us all to remember that we are citizens of the United States of America.

Check Your Reading

1. Name two places in Washington, D.C., where government leaders work.
2. What is a monument?
3. **GEOGRAPHY SKILL:** Look at the map on pages 268-269. Name a building located in C-8.
4. **THINKING SKILL:** List in correct order the places Christina and her family visit.

IMPORTANT EVENTS

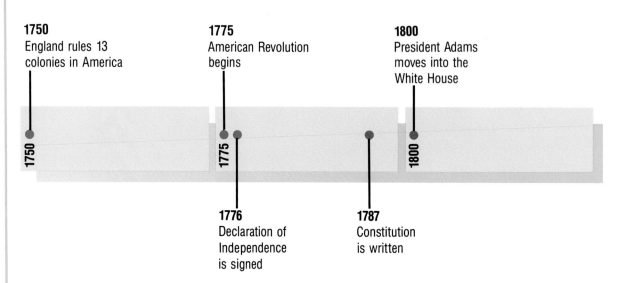

1750
England rules 13
colonies in America

1775
American Revolution
begins

1800
President Adams
moves into the
White House

1750

1775

1800

1776
Declaration of
Independence
is signed

1787
Constitution
is written

PEOPLE TO KNOW

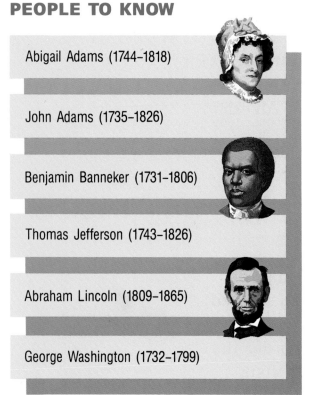

Abigail Adams (1744–1818)

John Adams (1735–1826)

Benjamin Banneker (1731–1806)

Thomas Jefferson (1743–1826)

Abraham Lincoln (1809–1865)

George Washington (1732–1799)

IDEAS TO REMEMBER

- The colonies fought the American Revolution to become independent.
- The Constitution organizes our country's government into three parts—Congress, the President, and the Supreme Court.
- Benjamin Banneker helped to plan Washington, D.C., our country's capital.
- The Capitol, the White House, and the many monuments are some of the places people can visit in Washington, D.C.

REVIEWING VOCABULARY

Capitol   monument
Congress   President
Constitution

Number a sheet of paper from 1 to 5. For each word on the list above, write a sentence using the word correctly. The sentence should show that you know what the word means.

REVIEWING FACTS

Number a sheet of paper from 1 to 5. Read each sentence below. If the sentence is true, write **T** next to the number. If it is false, rewrite the sentence to make it true.

1. The American Revolution was fought to free the American colonies from France.
2. The Constitution was signed on the Fourth of July.
3. Washington, D.C., is the capital of the United States.
4. John Adams worked from Pierre L'Enfant's plans to build our country's capital.
5. The flag is a symbol of our country.

((⟹ WRITING ABOUT MAIN IDEAS

1. **Writing Directions:** Look at the map on pages 268–269. Explain how to get by car from the White House to the Lincoln Memorial. Use words like *straight, north,* and *south.*
2. **Writing About a Song:** Review the song "Revolutionary Tea" on page 253. Write what the song means.

BUILDING SKILLS: READING GRID MAPS

Use the map on pages 268–269 to answer these questions.
1. How would you find **B-2** on a grid map?
2. In what square of the grid is the Capitol located?
3. What building is in **B-4**?
4. Why is it helpful to know how to read a grid map?

STUDYING YOUR COMMUNITY

Design a float for a Fourth of July parade in your community. Plan how it will look. Try to decide what materials you need to make it. Draw a picture of it.

REVIEWING VOCABULARY

Capitol	monument
citizen	President
Congress	property
Constitution	tax
mayor	volunteer

Number a sheet of paper from 1 to 10. Beside each number write a sentence using one of the words from the list above. The sentence should show that you know what the word means.

◀◤ WRITING ABOUT THE UNIT

1. **Writing a Paragraph:** Write a paragraph that compares the job of President with the job of mayor. Tell at least one way in which the jobs are the same and at least one way in which they are different.

2. **Writing a Tour Guide's Speech:** Imagine you are a tour guide in Washington, D.C. Your job is to show people interesting places in the city and to tell them about each place. Choose two places you would take people to see. Write the speech you would give at each place.

3. **Writing About Volunteering:** What type of volunteer work might you like to do now or when you get older? Write a paragraph telling the type of volunteer work you would like to do and why.

ACTIVITIES

1. **Interviewing Volunteers:** Interview at least two people in your community who work as volunteers. Ask them what they do and how they first started as a volunteer. Also ask them why they do volunteer work. Report what you find out to the class.

2. **Working Together to Prepare a Musical Show:** Put together a list of songs about the United States. Find out about the history of each song. Present the songs to the class. You may either sing them or play a record or tape of each one. Have one member of the group introduce each song by telling about its history.

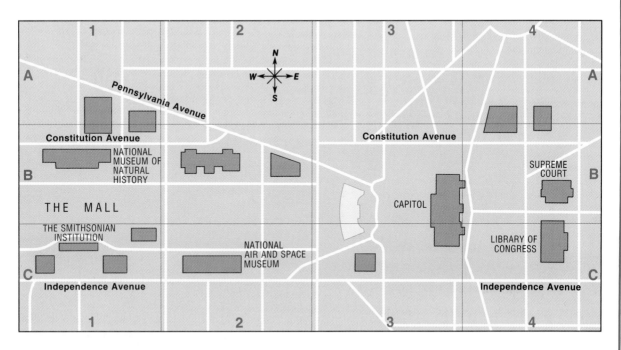

BUILDING SKILLS: READING GRID MAPS

Use the map to answer the following questions.

1. In what square is the Supreme Court?

2. Name a building in **C-1**.

3. Through what squares on the map does Independence Avenue run?

4. Why is it important to know how to use a grid map?

LINKING PAST, PRESENT, AND FUTURE

Once you are 18 years old, you will be able to vote to elect a President and members of Congress. You will also be able to vote to elect your community leaders. What kind of people will you vote for? Make a list of at least three qualities you think a leader should have. Beside each quality, write a sentence explaining why a leader should have it.

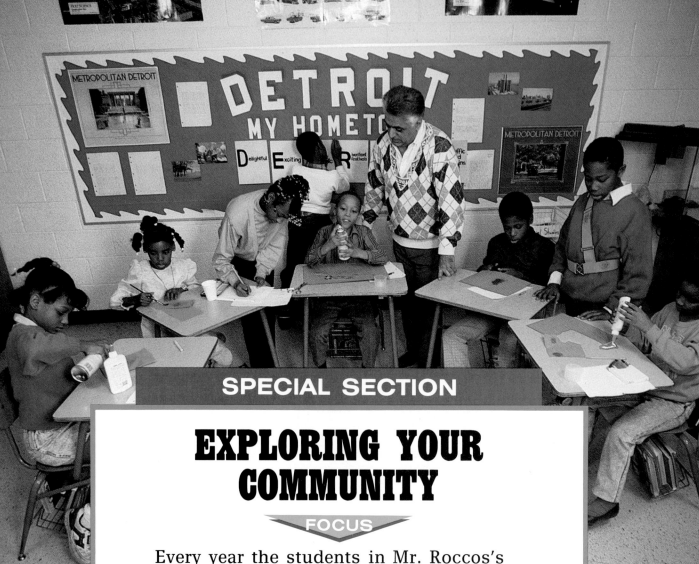

EXPLORING YOUR COMMUNITY

FOCUS

Every year the students in Mr. Roccos's class at Berry Elementary School in Detroit, Michigan, pick a class project. This year they wanted to do two things. They decided to make a guidebook to Detroit to tell new students what the community of Detroit is like. They also decided to put on a play about the history of their community.

In Part 1 of this section, you will see how the students made their guidebook. In Part 2 you will read their play.

GETTING STARTED

Everyone in the class wrote down his or her ideas for the guidebook. Mr. Roccos wrote all the ideas on the chalkboard. The list of ideas was used to make the table of contents for the book. Next to each idea, Mr. Roccos put the names of the students who wanted to work on that part of the book. The class asked the media teacher to help them type the guidebook on the computer. Now let's find out how the students got information for each part of the book.

TABLE OF CONTENTS

Important Facts About Our Community, by Jamaire

Our Community's History, by Rasheda

Government in Our City, by William

Community Services, by Crystal

Transportation, by Alveto

Working in Our Community, by Leon

Having Fun in Detroit, by Quincey, Bobbie, Antonio, and Adrienne

Why Our Community Is Special, by Kenyatta

IMPORTANT FACTS ABOUT OUR COMMUNITY
by Jamaire

Did you know?

1. Detroit is the largest city in the state of Michigan. Over one million people live in Detroit. It is the sixth largest city in the United States.

2. It is easy to get from Detroit to a foreign country. You can go by tunnel or bridge to Canada.

3. Detroit was built by the French along the Detroit River. This river is a strait, or narrow body of water. The French words for ''strait'' are *de troit*.

IMPORTANT FACTS ABOUT OUR COMMUNITY

Jamaire volunteered to find important facts about Detroit. He started by looking for information about Detroit in the encyclopedias in the school library.

The class also visited the public library. The librarian showed them a world almanac. An almanac is a book that contains facts on many subjects. At the public library the class also found five books for children about Michigan. They looked in the index of each book to find pages with information about Detroit. Jamaire used the almanac and books on Michigan to make the fact sheet.

OUR COMMUNITY'S HISTORY

Rasheda wrote about the history of Detroit. She got some special help from the community's history museum. The Detroit Historical Museum has information about the Indians of Michigan and about the history of Detroit. Mr. Roccos helped Rasheda make a list of questions to ask about Detroit's history. Then Rasheda and her older brother went to visit the museum and talk to a guide. Rasheda used the information she learned to make a time line about Detroit's history.

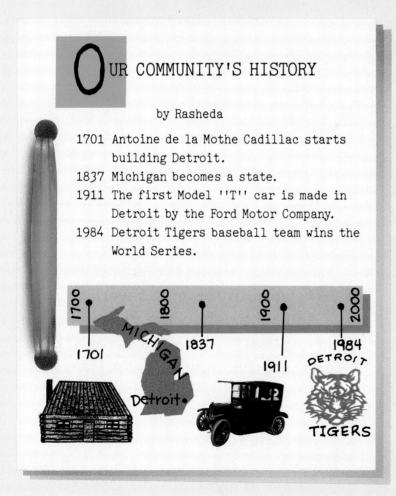

OUR COMMUNITY'S HISTORY

by Rasheda

1701 Antoine de la Mothe Cadillac starts building Detroit.

1837 Michigan becomes a state.

1911 The first Model ''T'' car is made in Detroit by the Ford Motor Company.

1984 Detroit Tigers baseball team wins the World Series.

1700   1800   1900   2000

1701   MICHIGAN   1837   1911   1984 DETROIT

Detroit•   TIGERS

GOVERNMENT IN OUR CITY

by William

Detroit has a mayor and city council. The mayor's name is Coleman Young. He has been the mayor of our city for over 15 years. The council has nine members. They are supposed to help each other. Sometimes they argue. You can read about that in the newspaper. Most of the time they work together to make Detroit a better place in which to live and work.

Coleman A. Young

GOVERNMENT IN OUR CITY

William wanted to learn about the government of Detroit. First he looked in the Detroit newspapers for stories about the mayor and the work of the city government. Then he called the mayor's office at city hall and asked for information about Detroit's government. William learned the name of the city council member from his part of the city.

COMMUNITY SERVICES

Crystal wrote about community goods and services. She started her part of the project by making a list of the stores in her part of the community. Then she wrote letters to the Detroit Chamber of Commerce and to the Detroit Convention and Visitor's Bureau. They sent her information about Detroit's schools and parks.

After Crystal wrote her page of the guidebook, she used the information she received to make a bulletin board display.

COMMUNITY SERVICES

by Crystal

Detroit has many stores. My mom likes them all. She shops at the Renaissance Center or at the Eastland Mall. On Saturdays we shop at a big outdoor market called the Eastern Market. Detroit also has many parks that everyone in the city can use. Lafayette Park and Chene Park are my favorites.

Our community also has a special service for students called the Homework Hotline. You can call a telephone number to get help with schoolwork. Of course, the teachers who answer the phones won't do your homework for you. But they will explain a math problem or tell you where to find information for a book report.

TRANSPORTATION

Alveto made a chart that showed all the different kinds of transportation found in Detroit. Then he wrote about his favorite kind of transportation.

TRANSPORTATION
by Alveto

Detroit has different kinds of public transportation. Here is a chart showing some of the different kinds. My favorite is the People Mover. It is an elevated train. You can ride it all over the downtown area. Each stop has interesting artwork to look at. I think you'd like riding on the People Mover.

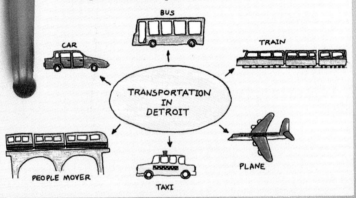

WORKING IN OUR COMMUNITY

Leon got information about places to work in Detroit from the Chamber of Commerce. He also talked to family members to ask them about their jobs.

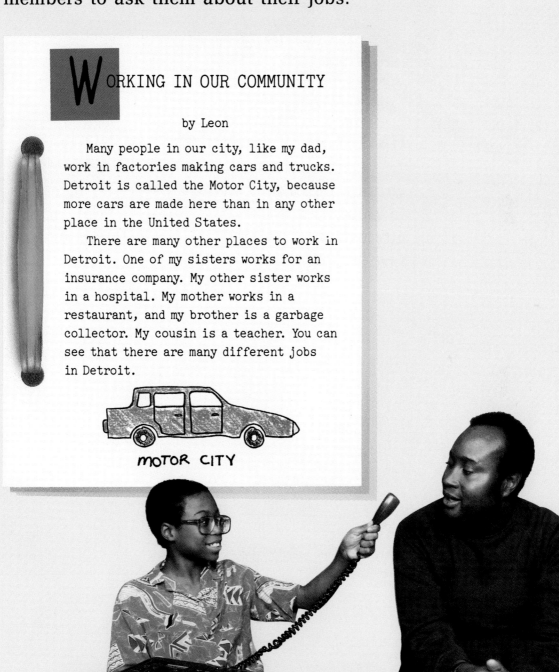

WORKING IN OUR COMMUNITY

by Leon

Many people in our city, like my dad, work in factories making cars and trucks. Detroit is called the Motor City, because more cars are made here than in any other place in the United States.

There are many other places to work in Detroit. One of my sisters works for an insurance company. My other sister works in a hospital. My mother works in a restaurant, and my brother is a garbage collector. My cousin is a teacher. You can see that there are many different jobs in Detroit.

MOTOR CITY

HAVING FUN IN OUR COMMUNITY

Quincey, Bobbie, Antonio, and Adrienne wrote about their favorite places to have fun in Detroit. Mr. Roccos brought a map of the city to class, and the students found their favorite places on the map.

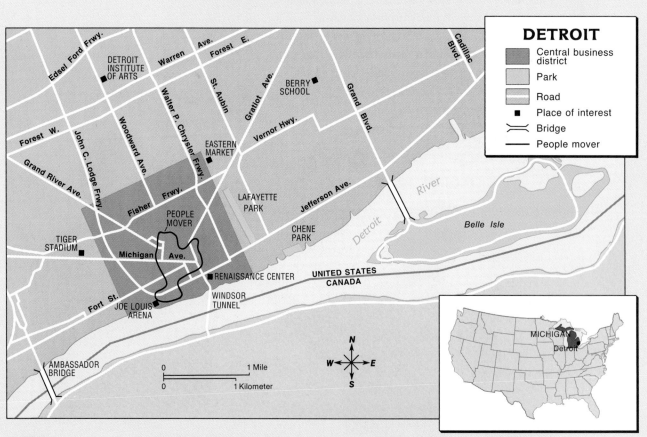

286

Having fun in Detroit

by Quincey, Bobbie, Antonio, and Adrienne

Here are some fun places to visit in Detroit.

Tiger Stadium I hope you like baseball, because we have a great team. The team's name is the Detroit Tigers. Tiger Stadium has a picture of a huge tiger on the front so you'll know you're in the right place.

Joe Louis Arena This winter my parents took me to the Joe Louis Arena to see ice skating. You can also see concerts there. My father told me this building was named for a famous boxer from Detroit who became the boxing champion of the world.

Detroit Institute of Arts This museum is one of the largest art museums in the United States. My favorite part of the museum is the African part. I saw face masks, arrows, and bowls. So if the weather is too hot or too cold, go to the museum and have a great day.

Belle Isle Belle Isle is a park located on an island in the Detroit River. If you go with your family, you can have a picnic and go fishing from the dock. You can swim in the river, and that's nice on a hot day. You can also visit the park's greenhouse. There you can see different plants from all over the world.

WHY OUR COMMUNITY IS SPECIAL

Kenyatta had the job of telling why Detroit is a special place to live. She talked to everyone in the class to find out why they thought Detroit was special. She read what everyone else had written in the guidebook. Reading this helped her decide what to write for this page of the guidebook.

WHY OUR COMMUNITY IS SPECIAL

by Kenyatta

Detroit is special because we live in it. People like us make it special by our work, our caring, and our attitudes. If we believe in our city and help one another, our city will remain a good community to live in. My teacher tells us that we are the mayors, doctors, teachers, and leaders of tomorrow. We have to take pride in ourselves and our city. Detroit is special in so many ways and so are we—its people

YOU CAN MAKE A DIFFERENCE

In this book, you have read about many people who made a difference. Joe Medalia helped the students at the Wilson-Pacific School. Now they have jobs and plenty of materials to help them learn about machines. Kathleen Correa helped her community. She brought together elders and children to keep alive Pueblo customs. You also read about the children who saved the salmon of Pigeon Creek. They cleaned up the creek so salmon could return there. Marion Stoddart fought pollution, too. She convinced people to clean up the Nashua River. Now the river is safe for people, fish, and animals.

These are only a few of the thousands of people who have helped their communities. Perhaps you know someone in your own community who saw a problem and solved it. It might even have been a young person like you.

When you look around your community, keep your eyes open for ways you can help. Is there a park that needs cleaning up? Does the library need to find a way to get more books? You might be able to solve one of these problems. You might think of other ways you can help your community. The important thing to remember is that *you* can make a difference.

A GIFT FOR GRANDMOTHER

by Wendy Vierow

Detroit began as a French trading post called La Ville d'Étroit (la vē dā′ twa). It was built by a man from France named Antoine de la Mothe Cadillac (an twan′ də la mōt ka dē yak). The Indians that lived near the community are called the Wyandot (wī ən dät). In this play you will read about some Wyandot children who visit Detroit.

THE PLAYERS

Tarhe—(tär′ hā)   Datasay—(dä′ tä sā)
Skahomat—(skä hō′ mät)   Cheyawe—(chā yä′ wā)
Father   Mother   Guard   Trader
Grandmother

PLACE: *Michigan*
TIME: *The Fall of 1705*

Tarhe, Datasay, Skahomat, and Cheyawe are outside their longhouse.

Datasay: The winter is coming. I think Grandmother needs a new blanket.

Tarhe: Let's give her one as a present.

Cheyawe: Where will we get a blanket?

Skahomat: We could make her one out of the beaver skins that Father brought us back from his last hunting trip.

Tarhe: I'd rather give her a bigger woolen blanket. Father told me they have many at the trading post at La Ville d'Étroit.

Datasay: That's a good idea. That would be a special gift.

Cheyawe: How will we get a woolen blanket?

Datasay: We have four beaver skins. If each of us gave the beaver skin that we got from Father to the French traders, we could get a blanket!

Tarhe: Let's ask Father and Mother if we can go to the trading post.

Datasay: I'll go inside and get them.

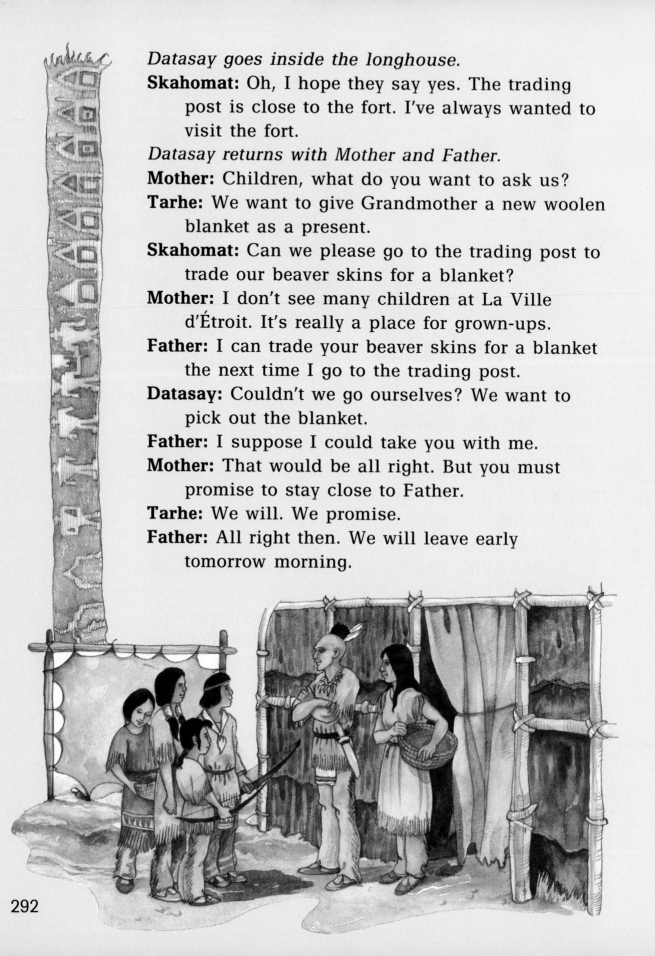

Datasay goes inside the longhouse.

Skahomat: Oh, I hope they say yes. The trading post is close to the fort. I've always wanted to visit the fort.

Datasay returns with Mother and Father.

Mother: Children, what do you want to ask us?

Tarhe: We want to give Grandmother a new woolen blanket as a present.

Skahomat: Can we please go to the trading post to trade our beaver skins for a blanket?

Mother: I don't see many children at La Ville d'Étroit. It's really a place for grown-ups.

Father: I can trade your beaver skins for a blanket the next time I go to the trading post.

Datasay: Couldn't we go ourselves? We want to pick out the blanket.

Father: I suppose I could take you with me.

Mother: That would be all right. But you must promise to stay close to Father.

Tarhe: We will. We promise.

Father: All right then. We will leave early tomorrow morning.

Early the next morning, Father, Tarhe, Datasay, Skahomat, and Cheyawe walk to La Ville d'Étroit.

Father: Did you see the farms outside the fort? Like us, the French are farmers as well as hunters. They raise wheat and corn here.

Tarhe: Do we trade inside the fort?

Father: No. We trade outside of the fort.

Cheyawe: Oh. I was hoping to see the town.

Father: If you like, you can look through the gates. I'm friends with the guard.

Skahomat: Oh could we? That would be great!

Father: Of course.

The Guard enters.

Guard: Hello. Good to see you. How are you?

Father: Fine. These are my children.

Guard: It's nice to meet you.

Father: They'd like to see inside the fort.

Guard: Well, come and take a look.

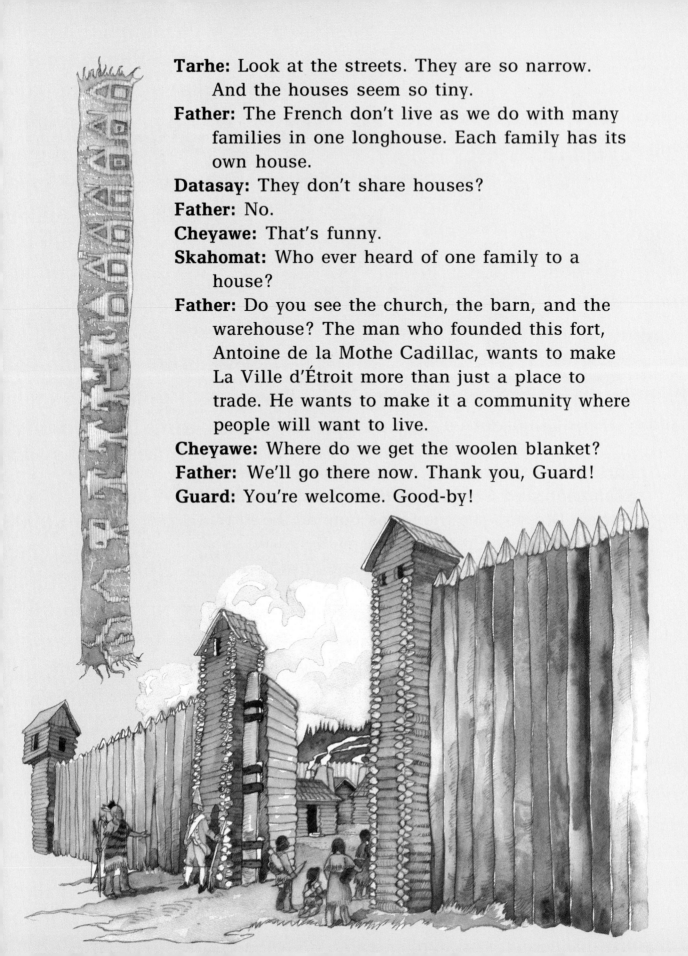

Tarhe: Look at the streets. They are so narrow. And the houses seem so tiny.

Father: The French don't live as we do with many families in one longhouse. Each family has its own house.

Datasay: They don't share houses?

Father: No.

Cheyawe: That's funny.

Skahomat: Who ever heard of one family to a house?

Father: Do you see the church, the barn, and the warehouse? The man who founded this fort, Antoine de la Mothe Cadillac, wants to make La Ville d'Étroit more than just a place to trade. He wants to make it a community where people will want to live.

Cheyawe: Where do we get the woolen blanket?

Father: We'll go there now. Thank you, Guard!

Guard: You're welcome. Good-by!

The Guard leaves. Father, Tarhe, Datasay, Skahomat, and Cheyawe walk to the trading post.

Skahomat: Are all the people here friendly?

Father: Most of them. The French try to work together with us. By trading, we get the goods we need, and the French get the beaver skins they need to make coats, hats, and gloves.

The Trader enters.

Datasay: We'd like to trade these four beaver skins for a woolen blanket.

Trader: I see you know the price of blankets. Which blanket would you like?

Tarhe: I think Grandmother would like this red one! She likes red because it's the color of the sky when the sun rises and sets.

Datasay: I guess we'll take the red one.

Trader: That would have been my choice, too. Here's your blanket.

Datasay: And here are your beaver skins.

Skahomat: Grandmother will love this!

The Trader leaves. Father, Tarhe, Datasay, Skahomat, and Cheyawe walk back to their village.

Skahomat: Grandmother! Are you home?

Grandmother enters.

Grandmother: Hello, children.

Cheyawe: Grandmother, we brought you a present!

Grandmother: Oh, you did?

Datasay: Yes—a red woolen blanket!

Grandmother: How beautiful! It's just what I needed! Thank you so much!

Tarhe: It's from all of us. We traded our beaver skins for it.

Cheyawe: And we even went to La Ville d'Étroit to trade for it!

Grandmother: Well, thank you so much for this beautiful gift. I will think of you every time I use it on the cold winter nights to come.

REFERENCE SECTION

ATLAS

WESTERN HEMISPHERE

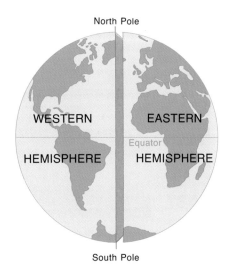

EASTERN HEMISPHERE

NORTHERN HEMISPHERE

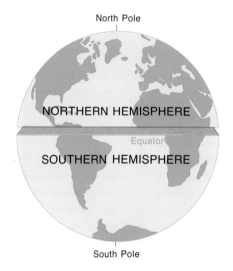

SOUTHERN HEMISPHERE

THE WORLD
Political

ARCTIC OCEAN

GREENLAND
(DENMARK)

ALASKA
(U.S.)

CANADA

**NORTH
AMERICA**

PACIFIC
OCEAN

UNITED STATES

AZORES
(PORT.)

ATLANTIC
OCEAN

BERMUDA

MEXICO

See inset below

HAWAII (U.S.)

CAPE
VERDE

Caribbean Sea

VENEZUELA   GUYANA
SURINAME
FRENCH GUIANA
COLOMBIA

Equator

GALAPAGOS
ISLANDS
(ECUADOR)   ECUADOR

**SOUTH
AMERICA**

PERU

BRAZIL

WESTERN
SAMOA

BOLIVIA

TONGA

PARAGUAY

EASTER ISLAND
(CHILE)

CHILE

URUGUAY

ARGENTINA

PACIFIC
OCEAN

FALKLAND ISLANDS
(U.K.)

ANTARCTICA

Central America
and West Indies

Gulf of Mexico

BAHAMAS

ATLANTIC
OCEAN

CUBA

MEXICO

DOMINICAN
REPUBLIC

PUERTO RICO (U.S.)

HAITI

VIRGIN ISLANDS (U.K.)
ST. CHRISTOPHER AND NEVIS
ANTIGUA AND BARBUDA

BELIZE

JAMAICA

VIRGIN
ISLANDS
(U.S.)

GUADELOUPE (FR.)

GUATEMALA

DOMINICA
MARTINIQUE (FR.)

HONDURAS

Caribbean   Sea

SAINT LUCIA
BARBADOS

EL SALVADOR

N

SAINT VINCENT AND
THE GRENADINES

PACIFIC
OCEAN

NICARAGUA

W   E

NETHERLAND ANTILLES
(NETH.)

GRENADA

S

TRINIDAD
AND TOBAGO

COSTA
RICA

VENEZUELA

0   250   500 Miles

PANAMA

SOUTH AMERICA

0   250   500   750 Kilometers

COLOMBIA

GUYANA

SURINAME

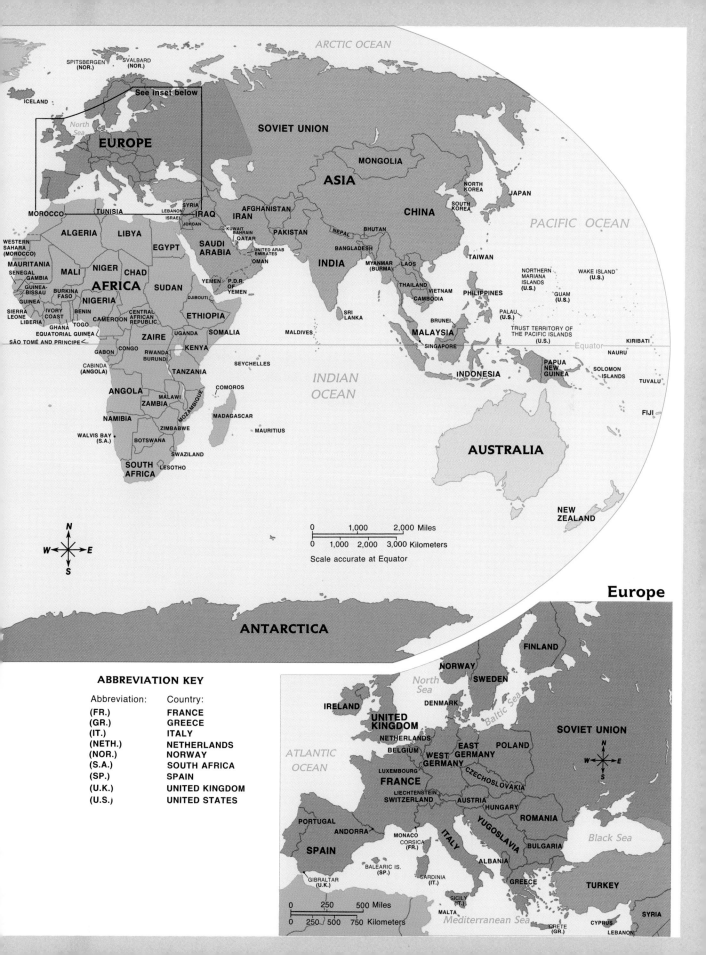

ALASKA

Nome
Fairbanks
Yukon River
CANADA
Anchorage
Juneau
PACIFIC OCEAN
ARCTIC OCEAN

0 250 500 Miles
0 250 500 750 Kilometers

CANADA

Seattle
WASHINGTON
Olympia
Spokane

Great Falls
Helena
Missouri   River
MONTANA
Billings

Portland
Salem
Eugene
OREGON

IDAHO
Boise

Snake   River
Pocatello

WYOMING
Casper
Cheyenne

NEVADA
Reno
Carson
City

Ogden
Salt Lake City
Provo
UTAH

Denver
COLORADO
Colorado
Springs
Pueblo

San
Francisco
Oakland
Sacramento
San Jose

CALIFORNIA

Las
Vegas

Colorado

ARIZONA

Santa Fe
Albuquerque
NEW MEXICO

PACIFIC OCEAN

Los Angeles
Long Beach
San Diego

Phoenix

Tucson

El Paso

Rio Grande

MEXICO

Kauai
Oahu   Honolulu
Molokai
Maui
HAWAII
Hilo
Hawaii
PACIFIC
OCEAN

0 100 Miles
0 100 Kilometers

N
W   E
S

THE UNITED STATES
Political

⊛ National capital ★ State capital • Other city

0   100   200   300 Miles

0   100 200 300 400 Kilometers

303

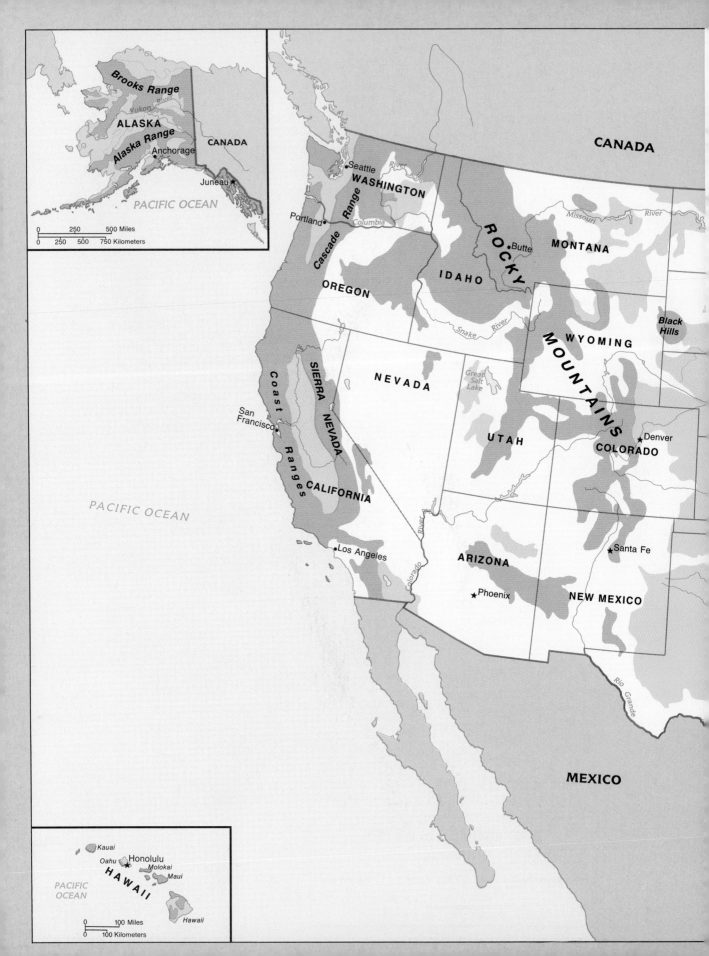

Brooks Range

ALASKA

Yukon River

Alaska Range

Anchorage

CANADA

Juneau ★

PACIFIC OCEAN

0   250   500 Miles

0   250   500   750 Kilometers

CANADA

Seattle

WASHINGTON

River

Portland

Columbia

R O C K Y

Missouri   River

Butte

MONTANA

Cascade Range

OREGON

IDAHO

Snake   River

WYOMING

Black Hills

Coast

SIERRA

NEVADA

Great Salt Lake

M O U N T A I N S

San Francisco

Ranges

NEVADA

UTAH

COLORADO

Denver ★

PACIFIC OCEAN

CALIFORNIA

Los Angeles

Colorado

ARIZONA

Santa Fe ★

Phoenix ★

NEW MEXICO

Rio

Grande

MEXICO

Kauai

Honolulu

Oahu   ★

Molokai

H A W A I I

Maui

PACIFIC OCEAN

Hawaii

0   100 Miles

0   100 Kilometers

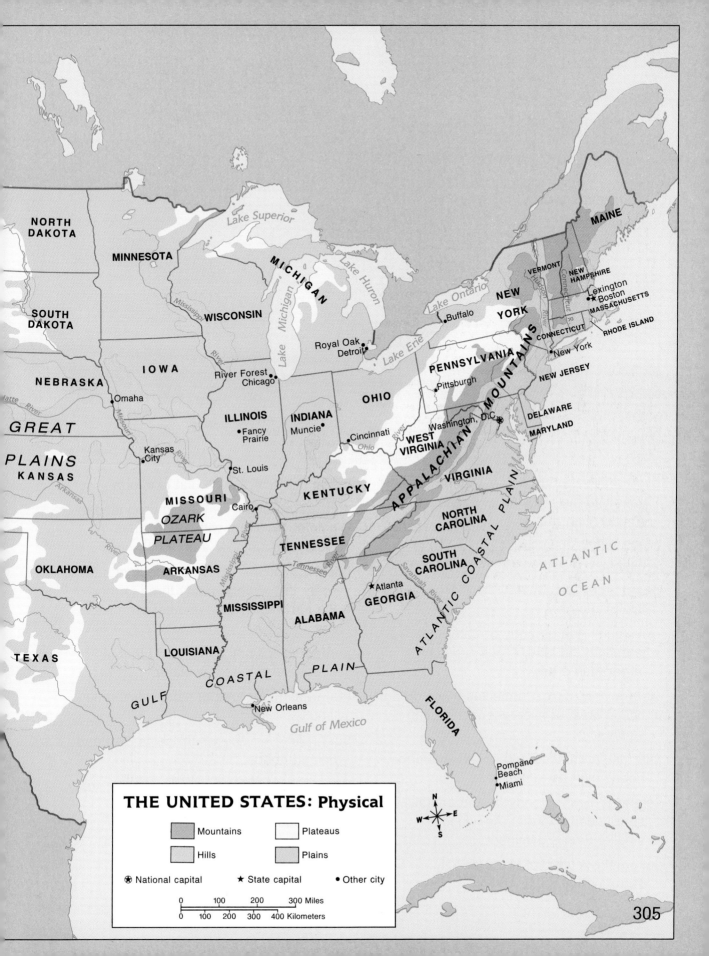

THE UNITED STATES: Physical

Legend:
- Mountains
- Plateaus
- Hills
- Plains
- ⊛ National capital
- ★ State capital
- • Other city

0 100 200 300 Miles
0 100 200 300 400 Kilometers

Labels on map:

NORTH DAKOTA
MINNESOTA
SOUTH DAKOTA
WISCONSIN
MICHIGAN
Lake Superior
Lake Huron
Lake Michigan
Lake Ontario
Lake Erie
NEBRASKA
IOWA
Omaha
Mississippi River
Missouri River
GREAT PLAINS
KANSAS
Kansas City
ILLINOIS
Fancy Prairie
INDIANA
Muncie
OHIO
Cincinnati
Ohio River
River Forest
Chicago
Royal Oak
Detroit
Buffalo
NEW YORK
PENNSYLVANIA
Pittsburgh
NEW JERSEY
Hudson River
Connecticut R.
VERMONT
NEW HAMPSHIRE
MAINE
Lexington
Boston
MASSACHUSETTS
CONNECTICUT
RHODE ISLAND
New York
DELAWARE
MARYLAND
Washington, D.C.
WEST VIRGINIA
VIRGINIA
APPALACHIAN MOUNTAINS
St. Louis
MISSOURI
OZARK PLATEAU
Cairo
KENTUCKY
TENNESSEE
Tennessee River
NORTH CAROLINA
SOUTH CAROLINA
Savannah River
ATLANTIC COASTAL PLAIN
OKLAHOMA
Arkansas River
ARKANSAS
MISSISSIPPI
ALABAMA
GEORGIA
Atlanta
Platte River
Arkansas River
TEXAS
LOUISIANA
COASTAL PLAIN
GULF
New Orleans
Gulf of Mexico
FLORIDA
Pompano Beach
Miami
ATLANTIC OCEAN

N
W E
S

305

DICTIONARY OF
GEOGRAPHIC TERMS

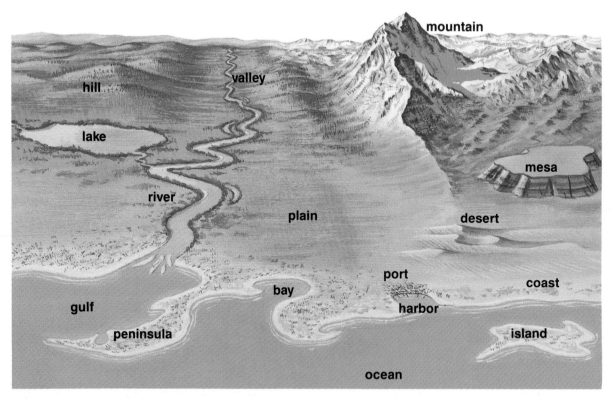

bay (bā) Part of a body of water that goes into the land. A bay is usually smaller than a gulf.

coast (kōst) The land along a sea or ocean.

desert (dez′ ərt) A very dry place where few plants grow.

gulf (gulf) A large body of water that goes into the land. A gulf is usually larger than a bay.

harbor (här′ bər) A protected place on an ocean, sea, or river where ships can safely stay.

hill (hil) A rounded and raised landform; not as high as a mountain.

island (ī′ lənd) A body of land entirely surrounded by water. An island is smaller than a continent.

lake (lāk) A body of water entirely surrounded by land.

mesa (mā′ sə) A high, flat landform.

mountain (mount′ ən) A high rounded or pointed landform with steep sides. A mountain is higher than a hill.

ocean (ō′ shən) The whole body of salt water that covers nearly three fourths of the earth's surface; another term for *sea*.

peninsula (pə nin′ sə lə) Land that is nearly surrounded by water.

plain (plān) An area of flat or almost flat land.

port (pôrt) A place where ships load and unload goods.

river (riv′ ər) A large stream of water that flows across the land and usually empties into a lake, an ocean, or another river.

valley (val′ ē) An area of low land between hills or mountains.

306

GAZETTEER

The Gazetteer is a geographical dictionary that will help you to pronounce and locate the places you have read about in this book. The page number tells you where each place appears on a map.

PRONUNCIATION KEY

a	cap	êr	clear	oi	coin	ü	moon
ā	cake	hw	where	ôr	fork	ū	cute
ä	father	i	bib	ou	cow	ûr	term
är	car	ī	kite	sh	show	ə	about, taken,
âr	dare	ng	song	th	thin		pencil, apron,
ch	chain	o	top	th	those		helpful
e	hen	ō	rope	u	sun	ər	letter, dollar,
ē	me	ô	saw	ù	book		doctor

A

Africa (af′ ri kə) A continent located in the Eastern and Southern hemispheres. (p. 6)

Allegheny River (al ə gā′ nē riv′ ər) A river near Pittsburgh, Pennsylvania, that joins with the Monongahela River to form the Ohio River. (p. 212)

Antarctica (ant ärk′ ti kə) A continent in the Southern Hemisphere. (p. 6)

Arctic Ocean (ärk′ tik ō′ shən) A large body of water located in the Northern Hemisphere. (p. 6)

Asia (ā′ zhə) A continent in the Eastern and Northern hemispheres. (p. 6)

Atlanta (at lan′tə) The capital and largest city in Georgia. (p. 176)

Atlantic Ocean (at lan′ tik ō′ shən) A large body of salt water located to the east of North America and South America, and west of Europe and Africa. (p. 6)

Austell (ô stel′) A suburb that is part of the Atlanta, Georgia, urban area. (p. 176)

Australia (ôs tral′ yə) A continent that is in the Southern and Eastern hemispheres. (p. 6)

B

Baltimore (bôl′ tə môr) A large city in Maryland. (p. 152)

Beijing (bā′ jing) Capital of China. (p. 224)

Boston (bôs′ tən) A large city in Massachusetts. (p. 152)

C

Canada (kan′ ə də) A country that is the northern neighbor of the United States. (p. 144)

Cape Cod Bay (kāp kod bā) A body of water near Massachusetts that is part of the Atlantic Ocean. (p. 98)

Castillo de San Marcos (ka stē′ yō   dā san mär′ kōs) A fort built by the Spanish in St. Augustine, Florida. (p. 90)

Chicago (shi kä′ gō) A city in Illinois. It is the third-largest city in the United States. (p. 152)

China (chī′ nə) A large country on the continent of Asia. (pp. 300–301)

Chinatown (chī′ nə   toun) A neighborhood in San Francisco. (p. 201)

Cincinnati (sin sə nat′ ē) A large city in Ohio. (p. 152)

Cleveland (klēv′ land) A large city in Ohio. (p. 152)

Columbus (kə lum′ bəs) A large city in Ohio. (p. 152)

D

Dallas (dal′ əs) A large city in Texas. (p. 152)

Denver (den′ vər) A large city near the Rocky Mountains in Colorado. Denver began as a mining community. (p. 152)

Detroit (di troit′) A large city in Michigan. (p. 286)

E

Embarcadero (em bär kə de′ rō) The part of San Francisco where the city's port is located. (p. 201)

England (ing′ lənd) Part of the United Kingdom an island country off the continent of Europe. (p. 183)

Equator (i kwā′ tər) An imaginary line halfway between the North Pole and South Pole, that goes completely around the earth. (p. 5)

Estevan (es′ tə van) A rural, wheat-farming community in Saskatchewan, Canada. (p. 144)

Europe (yür′ əp) A continent in the Eastern and Northern hemispheres. (p. 6)

F

Fancy Prairie (fan′ sē prâr′ ē) A farming community in Illinois. (pp. 304–305)

Forbidden City (fôr bid′ ən   sit′ ē) A part of the city of Beijing, China. (p. 224)

G

Golden Gate (gold′ ən gāt) A body of water that connects San Francisco Bay with the Pacific Ocean. (p. 194)

Golden Gate Park (gold′ ən   gāt   pärk) A park in the western part of the city of San Francisco. (p. 201)

Great Lakes (grāt   lāks) Five large bodies of water in North America. The lakes are: Huron, Ontario, Michigan, Erie, and Superior. (p. 152)

Great Plains (grāt   plānz) Large area in the middle of the United States of flat, grassy land. (pp. 304–305)

Gulf of Mexico (gulf   ov   meks′ ə kō) A large body of water that is part of the Atlantic Ocean. It is near the southeastern part of the United States. (p. 35)

H

Honolulu (hon ə lü′ lü) The capital and largest city in Hawaii. (p. 152)

Houston (hū′ stən) The fourth-largest city in the United States. It is located in Texas. (p. 152)

GAZETTEER

I

Indian Ocean (in′ dē ən ō′ shən) A large body of water located east of Africa. (p. 6)

J

Jacksonville (jak′ sən vil) A large city in Florida. (p. 152)

Juneau (jü′ nō) A city in Alaska. (pp. 302–303)

K

Kenya (ken′ yə) A country located in the eastern part of the continent of Africa. (p. 204)

L

Lake Erie (lāk ēr′ ē) One of the five Great Lakes. (p. 152)

Lake Huron (lāk hyùr′ ən) One of the five Great Lakes. (p. 152)

Lake Michigan (lāk mish′ ə gən) One of the five Great Lakes. (p. 152)

Lake Ontario (lāk on ter′ ē ō) One of the five Great Lakes. (p. 152)

Lake Superior (lāk sə pēr′ ē ər) The largest of the five Great Lakes. (p. 152)

Lexington (lek′ sing tən) A town in Massachusetts where the first shots of the American Revolution were fired. (pp. 304–305)

London (lun′ dən) The largest city and capital of England. (p. 183)

Los Angeles (lôs an′ jə ləs) The second largest city in the United States. It is located in California. (p. 152)

M

Memphis (mem′ fis) A city in Tennessee located on the Mississippi River. (p. 35)

Mesa Verde National Park (mā′ sə vâr′ dā nash′ ən əl pärk) A national park in Colorado where tourists can see the places where the Anasazi once lived. (p. 72)

Mexico (mek′ si kō) A country that borders the United States to the south. (pp. 300–301)

Mexico City (mek′ si kō sit′ ē) Capital of Mexico and its largest city. (p. 166)

Mission District (mish′ ən dis′ trikt) A neighborhood in San Francisco. (p. 201)

Mississippi River (mis ə sip′ ē riv′ ər) The longest river in the United States. (p. 35)

Mombasa (mom bä′ sə) A port city on the Indian Ocean in Kenya. (p. 204)

Monongahela River (mə nong gə hē′ lə riv′ ər) A river near Pittsburgh, Pennsylvania, that joins with the Allegheny River to form the Ohio River. (p. 212)

Muncie (mun′ sē) A city in Indiana. (pp. 304–305)

a cap; ā cake; ä father; är car; âr dare; e hen; ē me; êr clear; i bib; ī kite; o top; ō rope; ô saw; oi coin; ôr fork; ou cow; u sun; ù book; ü moon; ū cute; ûr term; ə about, taken, pencil, apron, helpful; ər letter, dollar, doctor

GAZETTEER

N

Nairobi (nī rō′ bē) The capital and largest city in Kenya. (p. 204)

New Orleans (nü ôr′ lē ənz) A large city in Louisiana. (p. 152)

New York City (nü yôrk sit′ ē) The largest city in the United States. It is in New York. (p. 152)

North America (nôrth ə mer′ i kə) A continent in the Northern and Western hemispheres. (p. 6)

North Beach (nôrth bēch) A neighborhood in San Francisco. (p. 201)

North Pole (nôrth pōl) The place farthest north on the earth. (p. 5)

O

Ohio River (ō hī′ ō riv′ ər) A river near Pittsburgh, Pennsylvania, that is formed when the Allegheny and Monongahela rivers join. (p. 212)

P

Pacific Ocean (pə sif′ ik ō′ shən) A large body of water located to the west of the United States. (p. 6)

Philadelphia (fil ə del′ fē ə) A large city in eastern Pennsylvania. (p. 152)

Phoenix (fē niks′) A large city in Arizona. (p. 152)

Pittsburgh (pits′ burg) A large city located in western Pennsylvania. (p. 221)

Plymouth (plim′ əth) A community started by the Pilgrims in Massachusetts. (p. 98)

Plymouth Bay (plim′ əth bā) A small body of water near Massachusetts on which Plymouth is located. (p. 98)

Pompano Beach (pom′ pə nō bēch) A community on the coast of the Atlantic Ocean in Florida. (pp. 304–305)

Puget Sound (pū′ jit sound) A body of water that is part of the Pacific Ocean. It is near Seattle, Washington. (p. 160)

R

Richmond (rich′ mənd) A suburb that is part of the London, England, urban area. (p. 183)

River Forest (riv′ ər fôr′ ist) A suburb that is part of the Detroit, Michigan, urban area. (pp. 304–305)

Rocky Mountains (rok′ ē mount′ ənz) Mountains found in the western part of North America. (p. 35)

Royal Oak (roi′ əl ōk) A community in Michigan. (pp. 304–305)

St. Augustine (sānt ô′ gəs tēn) A community in Florida started by people from Spain. It is the oldest community in the United States started by people from Europe. (p. 90)

San Agustin Antiguo (san ô gus′ tin an tē′ gwō) The oldest part of St. Augustine, Florida. (p. 90)

San Antonio (san an tō′ nē ō) A large city in Texas. (p. 152)

San Diego (san dē ā′ gō) A large city in California. (p. 152)

San Francisco (san frən sis′ kō) A large city in California. It is located on the Pacific Ocean. (p. 201)

San Francisco Bay (san frən sis′ kō bā) A body of water located east of San Francisco. (p. 194)

GAZETTEER

San Jose (san hō zā′) A large city in California. (p. 152)

Saskatchewan (sas kach′ ə won) A province in the central part of Canada. (p. 144)

Seattle (sē at′ əl) A large city in Washington. (p. 160)

South America (south ə mer′ i kə) A continent located in the Western Hemisphere. (p. 6)

South Pole (south pōl) The place farthest south on the earth. (p. 5)

Spain (spān) A country located in Europe. (p. 86)

Tian An Men Square (tē′ an an men skwâr) A part of the city of Beijing. (p. 224)

Valders (vôl′ dərz) A dairy farming community in Wisconsin. (p. 135)

W

Washington, D.C. (wôsh′ ing tən dē sē) The capital of the United States. (pp. 268–269)

a cap; ā cake; ä father; är car; âr dare; e hen; ē me; êr clear; i bib; ī kite; o top; ō rope; ô saw; oi coin; ôr fork; ou cow; u sun; u̇ book; ü moon; ū cute; ûr term; ə about, taken, pencil, apron, helpful; ər letter, dollar, doctor

GAZETTEER

BIOGRAPHICAL DICTIONARY

The Biographical Dictionary tells you about the Key People you have learned about in this book. The Pronunciation Key tells you how to say their names. The page numbers tell you where each person first appears in the text.

PRONUNCIATION KEY

a	cap	êr	clear	oi	coin	ü	moon
ā	cake	hw	where	ôr	fork	ū	cute
ä	father	i	bib	ou	cow	ûr	term
är	car	ī	kite	sh	show	ə	about, taken,
âr	dare	ng	song	th	thin		pencil, apron,
ch	chain	o	top	th	those		helpful
e	hen	ō	rope	u	sun	ər	letter, dollar,
ē	me	ô	saw	u̇	book		doctor

Adams, Abigail (ad′ əmz), 1744–1818. The wife of John Adams. She wrote many letters that tell about life in early Washington, D.C. (p. 260)

Banneker, Benjamin (ban′ i kər), 1731–1806. Helped to build Washington, D.C., by remembering and redrawing the plans for the city. (p. 260)

Adams, John (ad′ əmz), 1735–1826. The second President of the United States and the first President to live in Washington, D.C. (p. 260)

Bradford, William (brad′ fərd), 1590–1657. Was a leader of the Pilgrims at Plymouth. (p. 104)

Carnegie, Andrew

(kär nā′ gē), 1835–1919. Became rich working in the steel industry, then gave away much of his money to build libraries and museums in Pittsburgh and throughout the country. (p. 222)

Menéndez de Avilés, Pedro

(mə nen′ dəs dā ov′ ə lās), 1519–1574. Menéndez came from Spain to start a colony at St. Augustine. (p. 85)

Jefferson, Thomas

(jef′ ər sən), 1743–1826. The writer of the Declaration of Independence and the third President of the United States. (p. 254)

Squanto

(skwän′ tō), ?–1622. An Indian who helped the Pilgrims at Plymouth by teaching them how to plant corn, and where to fish and hunt. (p. 103)

Lincoln, Abraham

(ling′ kən), 1809–1865. The sixteenth President of the United States. He helped to free many black slaves. (p. 271)

Washington, George

(wôsh′ ing tən), 1732–1799. The first President of the United States. He also led the Americans during the American Revolution. (p. 260)

BIOGRAPHICAL DICTIONARY

GLOSSARY

The glossary will help you to pronounce and understand the meanings of the Key Vocabulary in this book. The page number at the end of the definition tells where the word first appears.

PRONUNCIATION KEY

a	cap	êr	clear	oi	coin	ü	moon
ā	cake	hw	where	ôr	fork	ū	cute
ä	father	i	bib	ou	cow	ûr	term
är	car	ī	kite	sh	show	ə	about, taken,
âr	dare	ng	song	th	thin		pencil, apron,
ch	chain	o	top	th	those		helpful
e	hen	ō	rope	u	sun	ər	letter, dollar,
ē	me	ô	saw	ù	book		doctor

A

American Revolution (ə mer′ i kən rev ə lü′ shən) The war the American colonists fought with England to make the colonies an independent country. After winning the **American Revolution**, the American colonies became independent. (p. 254)

assembly line (ə sem′ blē līn) A line of workers who put together the parts of a product. Mr. Bartman works on an **assembly line** in a factory putting wheels on cars. (p. 163)

author (ô′ thər) A person who writes books, stories, plays, poems, or articles. Paul Schmidt is the **author** of the book about San Francisco. (p. 100)

B

bar graph (bär graf) A graph that uses bars of different lengths to show amounts. The **bar graph** showed the population of five states. (p. 156)

basic needs (bā′ sik nēdz) Things people must have to live, such as food, shelter, and clothing. Communities help people to meet their **basic needs**. (p. 25)

bay (bā) Part of a body of water that goes into the land. Many people like to fish in the **bay**. (p. 98)

C

capital (kap′ it əl) The city where leaders of a country or state meet and work. Washington, D.C., is the **capital** of the United States. (p. 166)

Capitol (kap′ it əl) The building located in Washington, D.C., where Congress meets. Members of Congress meet in the **Capitol**. (p. 267)

cardinal directions (kärd′ ən əl di rek′ shənz) The cardinal directions are north, east, south, and west. Michael used the compass rose to find the four **cardinal directions** on the map of the United States. (p. 7)

central business district (sen′ trəl biz′ nis dis′ trikt) A part of a city where most of the city's businesses, stores, and restaurants are located. The **central business district** is often the busiest part of a city. (p. 159)

citizen (sit′ ə zən) A member of a community or a member of a country. The **citizens** worked together to clean up the playground and park. (p. 245)

city council (sit′ ē koun′ səl) A group of people who make laws for a community. The **city council** meets every Tuesday. (p. 241)

climate (klī′ mit) The kind of weather a place has over a long time. Los Angeles, California, has a warm **climate**. (p. 44)

coast (kōst) The land next to an ocean. There are many fishing villages along the **coast**. (p. 194)

colonist (kol′ ə nist) A person who lives in a colony. The Pilgrims were **colonists** from England who built a community at Plymouth. (p. 85)

colony (kol′ ə nē) A community in one country ruled by people from another country. The king of Spain wanted to build a **colony** in Florida to help protect Spanish trade. (p. 85)

community (kə mū′ nə tē) A group of people working together, and the places where they live, work, have fun, and share special times. One of Jonathan's favorite places to have fun in his **community** is the skating rink. (p. 16)

commuter (kə mū′ tər) A person who travels back and forth from his or her

community to a city where he or she works. The subway was filled with many **commuters** traveling into the city. (p. 176)

compare (kəm pâr′) To see how things are alike. The teacher asked the class to **compare** the two pictures to see how they were alike. (p. 76)

compass rose (kum′ pəs rōz) A compass rose shows directions on a map. By using the **compass rose** on the map, Emma knew the city was north of the bay. (p. 8)

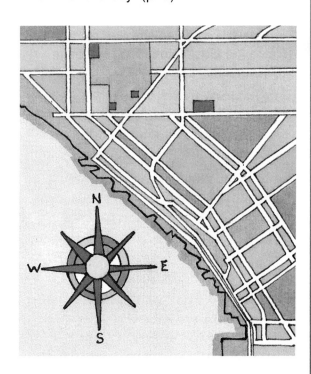

Congress (kong′ gris) The group of people who make the laws for our country. **Congress** meets in Washington, D.C. (p. 258)

Constitution (kon stə tü′ shən) The document that contains all the most important laws for our country. The laws for our country are written in the **Constitution**. (p. 257)

consumer (kən sü′ mər) A person who buys and uses products. **Consumers** can buy many different kinds of products in a supermarket. (p. 142)

continent (kont′ ən ənt) A very large body of land. The United States and Canada are both located on the **continent** of North America. (p. 7)

contrast (kən trast′) To see how things are different. Jill found the difference by **contrasting** the two photographs. (p. 76)

coquina (kō kē′ nə) A hard building material made up of shells of small sea animals. The Spanish used **coquina** to build the Castillo de San Marcos in St. Augustine. (p. 83)

culture (kəl′ chər) The way of life of a group of people. The language the Anasazi spoke and the food they ate were both part of their **culture**. (p. 60)

custom (kus′ təm) The special way a group of people does things. Having a picnic on the Fourth of July is a **custom** in Lucy's family. (p. 20)

D

dairy farm (dâr′ ē färm) A farm where cows are raised for their milk. Eric's family raises cows on their **dairy farm**. (p. 133)

Declaration of Independence (dek lə rā′ shən uv in di pen′ dəns) Thomas Jefferson wrote the Declaration of Independence to tell England that the colonists wanted to be an independent country. The signing of the **Declaration of Independence** is celebrated on the Fourth of July. (p. 254)

desert (dez′ ərt) A very dry place where few plants will grow. It does not rain very often in the **desert**. (p. 65)

dictionary (dik′ shə när ē) A book that gives the meaning of words. Andrew looked up the meaning of the word in the **dictionary**. (p. 101)

E

election (i lek′ shən) The way we choose our government leaders. The people voted for a new mayor in the **election**. (p. 237)

encyclopedia (en sī klə pē′ dē ə) A book or set of books that gives information about people, places, things, and events. Donna looked in the **encyclopedia** for information about the American Revolution. (p. 101)

equator (i kwā′ tər) An imaginary line, halfway between the North Pole and South Pole, that goes completely around the earth. The **equator** divides the earth into the Northern Hemisphere and the Southern Hemisphere. (p. 5)

GLOSSARY

F

factory (fak′ tər ē) A building where goods are made. Goods are often manufactured in a **factory**. (p. 163)

fiction (fik′ shən) Fiction is about imaginary people, places, and events. The **fiction** section of the library had many books on Paul Bunyan. (p. 100)

flow chart (flō chärt) A flow chart shows all the steps in an activity. Nancy used a **flow chart** to show what steps to follow to make fruit salad. (p. 146)

Forty-Niners (fôr′ tē nī′ nərz) A name for the people who went to California looking for gold in 1849. Most **Forty-Niners** who came to California looking for gold did not find any. (p. 197)

fuel (fū′ əl) Something that is burned to make heat or to provide power. Coal is an example of a **fuel**. (p. 213)

G

geography (jē og′ rə fē) The study of the landforms, bodies of water, climate, and natural resources of a place. It is also people, and the way they use land. Knowing about **geography** helps people decide how to use land. (p. 47)

goods (gudz) Things that people make or grow. When you buy things like apples and shoes you are buying **goods**. (p. 26)

government (guv′ ərn mənt) A group of people who lead a community, a state, or a country. The laws in the community are made by the **government**. (p. 237)

grid map (grid map) A map in which a grid, or a set of squares, is used to locate places. The **grid map** shows that the park is located in square C–4. (p. 264)

guide words (gīd wurdz) Words at the top of a page that tell what words are found on that page. The **guide words** on this page are *factory* and *harbor*. (p. 101)

H

harbor (här′ bər) A protected place where ships are safe from the ocean's waves. Many ships carrying goods from all over the world came into the city's **harbor**. (p. 82)

GLOSSARY

harvest (här′ vist) To pick crops that have been grown. The Pilgrims invited the Indians to a feast to celebrate the Pilgrim's **harvest**. (p. 105)

hemisphere (hem′ is fêr) One half of the earth. The United States is located in the Western **Hemisphere**. (p. 40)

history (his′ tər ē) The story of the past. Benjamin learned about some of our country's **history** when he visited Plimoth Plantation. (p. 74)

I

immigrant (im′ ə grənt) A person who comes to live in a new country. Many people who came to live in San Francisco were **immigrants**. (p. 201)

industry (in′ dəs trē) The many businesses that make one product. Many people in New York City work in the clothing **industry**. (p. 154)

intermediate directions (in tər mē′ dē it di rek′ shənz) Directions halfway between the cardinal directions. They are northeast, southeast, southwest, and northwest. The **intermediate directions** lines on the compass rose showed that the city was northwest of the river. (p. 42)

island (ī′ lənd) Land with water all around it. The only way Mary and Peter could get to the **island** was by boat. (p. 82)

K

kiva (kē′ və) A special underground room used by the Indians for praying. The park ranger told us that the Indians held special meetings in their **kiva**. (p. 69)

L

landform (land′ fôrm) The shape of the surface of the land. A mountain is one kind of **landform**. (p. 36)

law (lô) A rule for a community. Communities make many **laws** to help protect people and property. (p. 236)

M

map key (map kē) A map key explains what the symbols on a map stand for. The symbols were explained in the **map key**. (p. 10)

mayor (mā′ ər) The person elected by the people of a community to make sure laws are obeyed. The **mayor** makes sure a community's laws are obeyed. (p. 241)

mesa (mā′ sə) A landform made of rock and shaped like a high, flat table. The Indians grew corn on the top of the **mesa**. (p. 66)

monument (mon′ yə mənt) A building or statue made to honor a person or an event. Juan visited three **monuments** honoring important Americans on his trip to Washington, D.C. (p. 270)

museum (mū zē′ əm) A building where people can look at interesting things. We saw pottery at the **museum**. (p. 73)

N

national park (nash′ ə nəl pärk) Land that is set aside for all people in a country to enjoy. The **national park** was crowded with campers. (p. 72)

natural resource (nach′ ər əl rē′ sôrs) Something found in nature, such as trees, water, and animals, that people can use. Water, soil, and climate are examples of **natural resources** (p. 45)

nonfiction (non fik′ shən) Nonfiction is about real people, places, and events. Leo likes **nonfiction** books better than books about imaginary things. (p. 100)

North Pole (nôrth pōl) The place farthest north on the globe. We could see the **North Pole** on the globe. (p. 5)

O

ocean (ō′ shən) A large body of water. The fishing community is near the **ocean.** (p. 7)

P

pasture (pas′ chər) A field of grass on which animals feed. The farmer let the cows eat in the **pasture**. (p. 137)

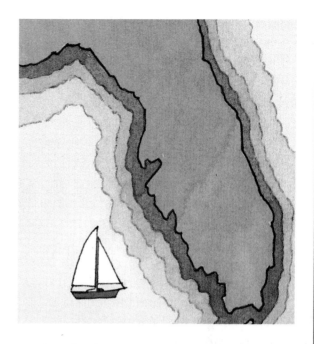

peninsula (pə nin′ sə lə) Land nearly surrounded by water. Florida is a **peninsula**. (p. 82)

plain (plān) Flat, grassy land. A **plain** is a good place for farming. (p. 36)

pollution (pə lü′ shən) Dirt that spoils land, water, or air. The city council made many laws that helped stop the air **pollution** problem. (p. 217)

population (pop yə lā′ shən) The number of people who live in a place. New York City has the largest **population** of any city in the United States. (p. 156)

port (pôrt) A place where ships load and unload goods. Manuel and his father went to the city's **port** to watch the ships being unloaded. (p. 152)

a cap; ā cake; ä father; är car; âr dare; e hen; ē me; êr clear; i bib; ī kite; o top; ō rope; ô saw; oi coin; ôr fork; ou cow; u sun; u̇ book; ü moon; ū cute; ûr term; ə about, taken, pencil, apron, helpful; ər letter, dollar, doctor

GLOSSARY

prairie (prâr′ ē) Flat land that was once covered with grass. The good soil of the **prairie** makes it one of the best places for wheat farming. (p. 144)

President (prez′ ə dent) The leader of the United States of America. People vote for **President** in an election every four years. (p. 258)

producer (prə dü′ sər) A maker of goods. The factory was a **producer** of airplanes. (p. 140)

product map (prod′ əkt map) A map that shows where crops are grown and goods are manufactured. Rebecca used a **product map** to find out if corn is grown in Kansas. (p. 214)

property (prop′ ər tē) Anything that people own. Public **property** such as parks and playgrounds can be used by all the people. (p. 236)

province (prov′ ins) A part of Canada; a province is like a state in the United States. Saskatchewan is a **province** in Canada. (p. 144)

public transportation (pub′ lik trans pər tā′ shən) Transportation that can be used by all the people in a community. Many of the commuters use **public transportation** to travel to their jobs in the city. (p. 178)

R

rural area (rür′ əl âr′ ē ə) A place where communities are surrounded by forest or farms. Most farms are located in **rural areas**. (p. 120)

S

scale (skāl) A scale on a map tells you the real size of places. By using the **scale**, Louis knew how many miles the city was from the river. (p. 38)

services (sûr′ vis iz) Work that helps other people. Teachers, doctors, and police officers all provide important **services** in communities. (p. 26)

South Pole (south pōl) The place farthest south on the earth. Shane looked at the bottom of the globe to find the **South Pole**. (p. 5)

suburb (sub′ ûrb) A community located near a big city. Michiko lives in the **suburbs**, and her parents travel to their jobs in the city each day. (p. 126)

subway (sub′ wā) An underground train. Melissa's mother takes a **subway** to her job. (p. 178)

Supreme Court (sə prēm′ kôrt) The most important court in the United States of America. The **Supreme Court** has to make many important decisions each year about our country's laws. (p. 258)

symbol (sim′ bəl) Anything that stands for something else. The American flag is a **symbol** of our country. (p. 10)

T

tax (taks) Money that people pay to support their government. The **tax** was needed to help pay for the new school building and the new road. (p. 242)

time line (tīm līn) A time line tells you when events happened, and the order in which they happened. The **time line** shows four important events in the history of Plymouth, Massachusetts. (p. 88)

tourist (tür' ist) A person traveling on vacation. The **tourists** spent their summer vacation visiting four states in the Southwest. (p. 91)

trade (trād) The buying and selling of goods. **Trade** was very important to the Spanish colonists who built St. Augustine. (p. 86)

transportation (trans pər tā' shən) The moving of people and products from place to place. Long ago, horses were used for **transportation** by many people in our country. (p. 173)

transportation map (trans pər tā' shən map) A map that shows you how you can travel from one place to another. The **transportation map** showed all the subway stops. (p. 180)

U

urban area (ûr' bən âr' ē ə) A city and the suburbs around it. Amy likes living in an **urban area** because there are many different museums to visit. (p. 127)

V

volunteer (vol ən têr') A person who does not get paid for the work he or she does. The **volunteers** helped to serve the food and to clean up at the community center picnic. (p. 244)

vote (vōt) To choose government leaders in an election. All 18-year-old citizens can **vote** in the election for mayor and city council members. (p. 237)

W

White House (hwīt hous) The place where the President of the United States lives and works. On her tour of Washington, D.C., Ana visited the Capitol building, the Lincoln Memorial, and the **White House**. (p. 267)

---

a cap; ā cake; ä father; är car; âr dare; e hen; ē me; êr clear; i bib; ī kite; o top; ō rope; ô saw; oi coin; ôr fork; ou cow; u sun; ù book; ü moon; ū cute; ûr term; ə about, taken, pencil, apron, helpful; ər letter, dollar, doctor

GLOSSARY

INDEX

Page references in italic type which follow an *m* indicate maps. Those following a *p* indicate photographs, artwork, or charts.

INDEX

CREDITS